The Quick-Reference
Handbook for
School Leaders

The Quick-Reference Handbook for School Leaders

P·C·P

Paul Chapman
Publishing

The Quick-Reference Handbook for School Leaders is an adaptation of
'*The Quick-Reference Handbook for School Leaders: A Practical Guide for
Principals* by the Ontario Principals' Council, first published by
Corwin Press, 2005

Adaptation © The National Association of Head Teachers 2006

First published 2007

Paul Chapman Publishing
A SAGE Publications Company
1 Oliver's Yard
55 City Road
London EC1Y 1SP

SAGE Publications Inc
2455 Teller Road
Thousand Oaks, California 91320

SAGE Publications India Pvt Ltd
B 1/I 1 Mohan Cooperative Industrial Area
Mathura Road, Post Bag 7
New Delhi 110 044

Library of Congress Control Number: 2006932533

A catalogue record for this book is available from the
British Library

ISBN 1-4129-3449-4   ISBN-13 978-1-4129-3449-7
ISBN 1-4129-3450-8   ISBN-13 978-1-4129-3450-3 (pbk)

Typeset by C&M Digitals (P) Ltd, Chennai, India
Printed in Great Britain by Athenaeum Press, Gateshead, Tyne & Wear
Printed on paper from sustainable resources

Contents

NAHT
The Association for all School Leaders

With a membership of over 28,000, the National Association of Head Teachers is the largest organization of its kind in Europe. Representing head-teachers, principals, deputies, vice-principals and assistant headteachers, it has provided over a century of dedicated support to its members. The union speaks with authority and strength on educational issues covering early years, primary, secondary and special sectors.

National Association of Head Teachers
1 Heath Square, Boltro Road, Haywards Heath, West Sussex, RH16 1BL
Tel: +44 1444 472472; email: info@naht.org.uk; website: www.naht.org.uk

O N T A R I O
P R I N C I P A L S'
C O U N C I L
Exemplary Leadership
in Public Education

The Ontario Principals' Council is a voluntary professional association for principals and vice-principals in Ontario's public education system. We believe that exemplary leadership results in outstanding schools and improved student achievement. To this end, we foster quality leadership through world-class professional services and supports. Through our ISO 9001 registered quality management system, the Ontario Principals' Council and its professional development division, Education Leadership Canada, strive to continuously achieve the organization's assertion that 'quality leadership is our principal product.'

Ontario Principals' Council
180 Dundas Street West, 25th Floor, TORONTO, Canada, M5G 1Z8
Tel: +1(416)322-6600 Fax: +1(416)322-6618 Website: www.principals.on.ca

Preface

The Quick-Reference Handbook for School Leaders is the product of a partnership between the National Association of Head Teachers (NAHT) and the Ontario Principals' Council (OPC). Our organizations share an active commitment to the support and development of excellent school leadership, which we believe to be the key to raising standards of achievement and thus enhancing the life chances of all learners. The *Handbook* is intended to be a first point of contact for those colleagues who feel they need help when facing challenging leadership and management situations, perhaps for the first time. To this end, it has been designed to be accessible, practical and comprehensive. We intend this to be the first of a number of joint ventures that will enable us to bring together expertise and experience from both sides of the Atlantic for the benefit of our respective members and for school leaders generally.

Out thanks are due to the following for their various contributions: Chris Batt; Dave Beresford; Kathy James; Tony Kemp; Michael Lloyd; Jan Myles; Mike Parkhouse; Pauline Smith; Karen Stevens; Claire Thompson; Rona Tutt and Carole Whitty.

Introduction

The Quick-Reference Handbook for School Leaders: An Overview

> I'm the new headteacher …
> What do I do now?

The Quick-Reference Handbook for School Leaders is designed primarily for new headteachers, but it is a useful resource for all headteachers and senior school staff. The *Handbook* does not separately describe headteacher and other senior leader responsibilities, primary and secondary issues, or management and leadership functions. The *Handbook* is designed to be a hands-on practical guide, wide-ranging, but not exhaustive. Please note that the *Handbook* is not legal advice. Headteachers and senior school staff, first and foremost, must follow their local authority and/or governing body policies and procedures.

Where the term *headteacher* is used this is taken to mean *headteacher, principal, deputy headteacher* and *assistant headteacher* or other *senior leader* who is required to deputize for the headteacher.

Where the term *parent* is used this is taken to mean *parent, carer* or *guardian*.

How to use the *Handbook*

The *Handbook* is organized so that you can quickly look up a specific topic in the index, or browse through the table of contents to identify areas of interest. It has 31 chapters, which are listed in the table of contents. It also includes a resource list   and references.

Any DfES, NCSL and Ofsted publications referred to in this book are available from the relevant website. DfES: www.dfes.gov.uk, NCSL: www.ncsl.org.uk, Ofsted: www.ofsted.gov.uk.

Icons

The *Handbook* is divided into five sections. Each section has an icon to identify the five major areas of the book:

⋕ Part 1   Organization and Management

◉ Part 2   Teaching and Learning

◉ Part 3   Behaviour and Discipline

((●)) Part 4   Health and Safety

Y Part 5   Looking After Yourself.

You will also find a series of icons within chapters that indicate the accompanying text is presented as:

✓ A checklist

→ An overview

TIPS Tips

→ Suggestions for getting started

📖 Further reading.

Text boxes

Three types of text boxes are used in the *Handbook*.

'At a glance' boxes

Each chapter in the *Handbook* is divided into subsections, which are also listed in the table of contents. At the beginning of every chapter, you will find an outline of the contents; an example is shown below.

At a glance

- Before the meeting

    Meeting planning checklist
    Sample meeting agendas

- During the meeting
- After the meeting

Shaded text boxes

Certain sections of text are highlighted in shaded text boxes, which contain information that reinforces the main message. Direct quotes are referenced at the bottom of the shaded box.

> 'When a teacher makes plans to become a headteacher, the long range goal is to make a difference in the lives of children.
>
>   Teachers become headteachers to be instructional leaders.'
>
>   (Alvy and Robbins, 1998, p. 37)

The voice of experience

More than 60 primary and secondary headteachers and senior school staff responded to the question: 'What piece of advice would you give to new head-teachers?' These are found at the end of each chapter in the voice of experience boxes.

HIRE WELL

Staffing decisions are critical.
If I could give only one piece of advice, it would be to hire well.

Words of wisdom: advice from new headteachers

Members of the *Handbook* focus group were asked what advice they would like to pass on to new headteachers. The members of this focus group were first year primary and secondary headteachers. See Chapter 31, 'Words of Wisdom'.

PART 1
Organization and Management

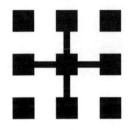

1 The Role of the Headteacher

At a glance

- Duties and responsibilities: an overview
- The headteacher's role
- Additional roles and skills: a quick overview

    Emotional intelligence: a key to effective leadership
    Roles
    Skills

- Your personal vision of your role as headteacher
- The role of the headteacher as legally defined

    1. *Responsibility guidelines*
    2. *Pupil safety*
    3. *Pupil education*
    4. *Pupil supervision*
    5. *Staff management*
    6. *Staff evaluation and development*
    7. *Staff cooperation*
    8. *School administration*
    9. *Access to school*
    10. *Site maintenance*
    11. *Community*
    12. *Governing body*
    13. *Reports to local authorities/Department for Education and Skills (DfES), if required*

⊙ Duties and responsibilities: an overview

A headteacher's principle duties are to:

- lead, organize and manage the school;
- maintain proper order and discipline in the school; and
- be in charge of, and supervise, the education of pupils.

- See 'The role of the headteacher as legally defined' in this chapter for an overview of the legal aspects of the headteacher's role.
- Check the DfES and teachernet websites regularly for updates to this legal definition.

Remember: Education websites are where many parents get their information about education: governornet, parents centre, National Confederation of Parent Teacher Associations (NCPTA), National Governors Association, and so on.

⊙ The headteacher's role

Headteachers, under the direction of their governing bodies, take a leadership role in the daily operation of a school. They provide this leadership by:

- demonstrating care and commitment to academic excellence and a safe teaching and learning environment
- holding everyone under their authority accountable for their behaviour and actions
- communicating regularly and meaningfully with all members of their school community.

In addition, headteachers are responsible for the organization and management of individual schools, including the budget assigned to the school. The headteacher is the senior professional and leads the teaching and learning provision in the school. In addition to any teaching duties, each headteacher is responsible for:

- determining the organization of the school and ensuring ongoing maintenance of the school buildings
- administering the school's budget
- placing pupils in appropriate classes
- ensuring that reports are sent to parents
- attending meetings, acting as a professional adviser at those meetings, considering recommendations, and reporting back on actions taken
- developing a safe school environment with the help of parents, staff, governors and the community.

All the above roles are carried out by the headteacher as he/she implements and operates the policies and procedures adopted by the governing body.

◉ Additional roles and skills: a quick overview

The following are a few ways to describe the roles and skills required of a headteacher.

Emotional intelligence: a key to effective leadership

School leaders bring their values, knowledge, experience and skill to their work each day. The understanding and appropriate application of emotional intelligence (EI) is key to effective leadership. As the challenges, demands and complexities of the headteacher's role increase, this competence will continue to be the foundation of dynamic, successful and effective leadership.

Emotional intelligence, unlike intelligence quotient (IQ), can be learned and enhanced. Headteachers, deputy headteachers and assistant headteachers are encouraged to read about and/or take training to assess and enhance their emotional intelligence.

The *five* components of emotional intelligence, together with their subscales, are as follows:

1. *Intrapersonal*: our ability to be aware of ourselves, to understand our strengths and weaknesses, and to express our thoughts and feelings non-destructively.

   - Independence
   - Self-actualization
   - Self-regard

- Emotional self-awareness
- Assertiveness

2. *Interpersonal*: our ability to be aware of others' emotions, feelings, and needs and to be able to establish and maintain cooperative, constructive and mutually satisfying relationships.

   - Interpersonal relationships
   - Social responsibility
   - Empathy

3. *Adaptability*: our ability to manage change, by realistically and flexibly coping with the immediate situation, effectively solving problems as they arise and anticipating future demands.

   - Problem-solving
   - Reality testing
   - Flexibility
   - Acting proactively

4. *Stress management*: our ability to manage emotions so that they work for us and not against us.

   - Impulse control
   - Stress tolerance

5. *General mood*: our ability to be optimistic, positive and sufficiently self-motivated to set and pursue our goals.

   - Happiness
   - Optimism
   - Self-confidence

Further reading

Goleman, D. (1995) *Emotional Intelligence.*
Goleman, D. (1998) *Working with Emotional Intelligence.*
Goleman, D., Boyatzis, R.E. and McKee, A. (2002) *The New Leaders: Transforming the Art of Leadership into the Science of Results.*
Stein, S. and Book, H. (2000) *The EQ Edge.*

Roles

As leader

1. Standards setter
2. Advocate
3. Climate builder
4. Communicator
5. Motivator
6. Negotiator
7. Organization developer
8. Planner
9. Researcher
10. Professional leader

Source: adapted from Newberry, 1996, pp. 32–40.

As manager

1. Interpersonal roles: figurehead, leader, person who liaises
2. Informational roles: monitor, disseminator, spokesperson
3. Decisional roles: entrepreneur, dispute resolver, resource allocator, negotiator

Source: adapted from Mintzberg, quoted in Straub, 2000, p. 2, fig. 1-1.

Skills

1. Interpersonal skills: leadership, sensitivity, motivation of self and others
2. Administrative skills: problem analysis, judgement, organizational ability, management
3. Communication skills: oral, written
4. Knowledge of self

Refer to the National Standards for Headteachers for a fuller statement.

Your personal vision of your role as headteacher

Consider these questions as you develop a personal vision:

- What are your duties and responsibilities under the Acts and regulations, policies and procedures?
- What tasks must you carry out?
- What professional roles must you play?
- What skills do you need?
- What principle(s) will guide you?
- What are your standards?

After a couple of hectic months on the job, one new headteacher started to develop this personal vision statement:

First, I'll consider what's in the best interest of the pupils.
I'll strive to promote academic excellence and continuous school improvement.
I'm responsible for the safety and well-being of pupils and staff, the education and discipline of pupils, and the organization and management of the school.

My personal vision of my job as a headteacher

What is your personal vision of your job as a headteacher? Whether you are a new headteacher or an experienced headteacher, it's important to be able to answer this question readily, for yourself and for others.

The role of the headteacher as legally defined

The role of headteachers and deputy headteachers is defined largely by statute and by the terms and conditions of their employment with their employer, the local authority (LA) and/or governing body. Most documents talk about the headteachers responsibility to implement governing body policies and to lead, manage and operate the provision of education.

Set out below are various categories of headteacher and deputy headteacher responsibilities. Some duties relate to more than one category and so are reproduced in more than one section. This summary is intended to provide an overview only, and does not purport to be all-encompassing.

The School Teachers' Pay and Conditions Document is updated annually and should be available in all schools. The Document contains definitive contractual requirements for teachers and headteachers.

1. Responsibility guidelines

(a) Maintain order and discipline in the school.
(b) Be responsible for the instruction and the education of pupils in the school.
(c) Ensure the health and safety of staff, pupils and visitors as far as is reasonably practicable.
(d) Inform parents, governors, staff, pupils, the LA and DfES (if necessary) about school matters, issues and actions.

2. Pupil safety

(a) Ensure that all reasonable health and safety issues are addressed in courses and activities for which the teacher is responsible.
(b) Report to the appropriate agency, usually the LA lead officer for child protection, when there are reasonable grounds to suspect child abuse, neglect or harm.
(c) Ensure care of pupils and property.

3. Pupil education

(a) Oversee, monitor and model effective pedagogy.
(b) Monitor and assess pupil progress.
(c) Ensure school development planning is focused on improved teaching and learning.

4. Pupil supervision

(a) Ensure supervision of pupils when the school buildings and playgrounds are open.
(b) Ensure supervision of pupils during the conducting of any school activity, on or off site; not including travel to and from school at the beginning and end of the school day, unless this involves the school's own transport.
(c) Ensure that staff carry out the supervisory duties and curriculum programme assigned by the headteacher and supply such information as the headteacher may require.

5. Staff management

(a) Monitor and evaluate the education provided by the school.
(b) Assign duties to the leadership team, middle managers and support staff. A deputy headteacher shall perform such duties as are assigned by

the headteacher. In the absence of the headteacher of a school, a deputy headteacher, where a deputy headteacher has been appointed for the school, shall be in charge of the school and shall perform the duties of the headteacher. (See School Teachers Pay and Conditions Document.)

(c) Monitor and evaluate the work of psychiatrists, psychologists, social workers, and other professional support staff where such persons are performing their duties in the school, but are not employees of the governing body.

6. Staff evaluation and development

(a) Carry out induction procedures for newly qualified teachers (NQTs) in conjunction with the LA; and provide induction for newly appointed (experienced) staff.

(b) Conduct performance management of all teachers annually as required by the 'appraisal' regulations.

(c) If a performance is unsatisfactory, the headteacher must:

    (i) document concerns

   (ii) consult regularly with their line manager regarding the teacher's performance and steps that may be taken to improve it

  (iii) provide feedback and recommendations to the teacher to help improve the teacher's performance

  (iv) ultimately, consider the need to use the official personnel procedures for capability if inadequacies persist.

7. Staff cooperation

(a) Ensure that senior staff and teachers display personal and professional qualities.

(b) Establish and maintain mutually respectful relationships with pupils, staff, governors and parents.

8. School administration

(a) Maintain pupil records including attendance.

(b) Review all school data at intervals, to inform strategic planning.

(c) Ensure all policies and codes of conduct are adhered to.

9. Access to school

(a) Manage visitors who come to the school and ensure security of the site.
(b) Liaise with health services staff or the County Medical Officer regarding staff, pupils or visitors who represent a health risk on site.
(c) Be aware of the ultimate legal powers to ban visitors who cause nuisance and disturbance to the annoyance of those lawfully present.

10. Site maintenance

(a) Monitor the condition and maintenance of property.
(b) Inspect the school premises regularly and make reports to appropriate governors and LA representatives.
(c) Provide appropriate facilities for education and other activities.

11. Community

(a) Promote and maintain close cooperation with community and business.
(b) Promote and maintain close cooperation with parents and guardians.

12. Governing body

(a) Act as leading professional to the governing body, and assist them in obtaining information, formulating policy and providing a strategic framework.
(b) Discuss with the governors codes of conduct, school policies and school action plans for improvement based on data, and monitoring of pupil progress.
(c) Consider recommendations and advice when determining action to be taken in response to discussions, and report back to the governors the results of the actions.

13. Reports to local authorities/DfES, if required

(a) Report to school improvement partners (SIPs), local authorities, DfES, Her Majesty's Inspectorate (HMI), Office for Standards in Education (Ofsted) and diocesan education officers, where appropriate.

ALWAYS PUT THE PUPILS FIRST

Always put the pupils first in any decision that you make. Let this be the philosophy upon which you structure the school.

Establish a strong vision that puts pupil well-being and achievement first, and use that as your guide when dealing with parents and staff.

2 Legal Framework

At a glance

- Hierarchical legislative framework: an overview

    Legislation
    Key agencies
    Individual schools: policies, procedures and rules

Hierarchical legislative framework: an overview

All of your day-to-day duties, responsibilities and activities are carried out within a hierarchical legislative framework:

Legislation (Acts of Parliament and statutory instruments)
↓
Good practice, advice and guidance = LA/DfES/ACAS, and so on
↓
Governing body policies

Legislation

Examples:

1. Education Acts and statutory instruments
2. Human rights legislation

3. Employment Acts
4. Other relevant Acts and regulations, for example, Health and Safety at Work Act 1974, Children Act 1989

Key agencies

- Local authorities may have operational policies and procedures for community schools.
- Dioceses may have similar for diocesan (voluntary aided) schools.
- The Advisory Conciliation and Arbitration Service (ACAS) may have advice on good personnel practise.
- Disability Rights Commission on issues of disability.
- Department of Transport on school bus issues.
- Home Office on drugs and criminal issues, and so on.

> In general, policies dictate what to do, and procedures describe in detail how to do it.

Individual schools: policies, procedures and rules

School policies and procedures

Individual school governing bodies create and implement their own policies and procedures, which must be consistent with national policies for schools, for example, the length of the school year or the admissions system. In community schools they will need to be consistent with local authority procedures.

School rules

Individual schools also establish their own rules with specific expectations for behaviour, accompanied by clear consequences. Rules may be specific to particular schools, but should follow general governmental and local governmental approaches. For example, pupils at one school may be allowed wide variations as regards school uniform, while at another the uniform is much more prescribed. Both schools must ensure that both genders are treated appropriately and to the same standard, and that religious and cultural differences are considered.

ALWAYS PUT THE PUPILS FIRST

Never take the easiest solution to a difficult problem; it is seldom the best solution.
Always do the hard thing, the right thing, the ethical thing.
Make sure all school decisions are made in the best interests of your pupils.

3 Negligence and Liability

At a glance

- First steps to reduce risk

    *Review policies and procedures from your local authority
    (for community schools) and your governing body (for all other schools)*

    Review, communicate and monitor school policies and procedures
    Develop the documentation habit
    Encourage staff to keep up to date

- Negligence: an overview of the concepts and issues

    Negligence
    Duty of care
    Standard of care

- Duty to provide adequate supervision of pupils

➔ First steps to reduce risk

You, the staff, the pupils, and their parents all desire and deserve a safe teaching and learning environment in the school.
The steps you take to promote a safe environment will reduce the risk of injury or loss.

Here are some initial steps you can take to reduce the risk of injury and loss, and thus reduce the risk of legal liability.

Review policies and procedures from your local authority (for community schools) and your governing body (for all other schools)

- It is critical to know and follow your employer's policies and procedures, especially those related to higher-risk activities, for example, field trips, administering medication to pupils, restraint, recruitment of staff, and so on.
- Your legal requirement is to ensure, so far as is reasonably practical the health and safety of yourself and others, to cooperate with your employer and to inform them of any serious risks.

Review, communicate and monitor school policies and procedures

Review

1. Do the school policies, procedures and practices follow the employer's policies and procedures?
2. Does the school handbook reflect the employer's policies?

Communicate

1. Inform staff, pupils and parents at the start of the school year and on an ongoing basis.
2. Discuss issues regularly with school staff, parents and volunteers/visitors.
3. Document staff discussions (for example, items on staff meeting agenda, references in staff meeting minutes).
4. File memos to staff, parents and volunteers.
5. Raise health and safety/risk issues at intervals with the governing body.

Monitor

1. Monitor and ensure compliance.
2. Document conversations you have with individual staff members regarding concerns and actions taken.
3. Be mindful of collective agreements and union relations.
4. For local authority schools, inform their health and safety staff of risk issues.

Develop the documentation habit

- Written records must be specific; note the date, time, place and people involved.
- Be accurate and factual, and record what was said.
- Be objective. Do not include personal opinions and value judgements.

> Staff in schools must be increasingly diligent about documenting all controversial phone calls, meetings and events.

Encourage staff to keep up to date

Encourage teachers to keep up to date on curriculum and safety issues by joining professional and subject associations.

⊙ Negligence: an overview of the concepts and issues

Negligence

Negligence is concerned with unintentional acts or omissions that may cause a loss or injury. In general, you will not be found liable for negligence unless it is proven that:

- there was a duty of care toward the plaintiff (for example, the pupils)
- there was a breach of the duty of care owed
- the breach was the proximate cause of the loss or injury
- there was actual damage or loss as a result of the injury.

> 'Negligence is the omission to do something which a reasonable man, guided upon those considerations which ordinarily regulate the conduct of human affairs, would do, or doing something which a prudent and reasonable man would not do.'
>
> (*Blyth* v. *Birmingham Water Works Co.,*
> as quoted in Brown, 1998, p. 102)

Duty of care

Headteachers, teachers, and local authorities owe a duty of care to their pupils; that is, a duty to ensure the pupils' safety and well-being. The old concept of 'in loco parentis' has now been replaced by the concept of duty of care as should be given by a comparable trained and experienced co-professional, that is, teacher. To compare school staff to parents is inappropriate as parents do not have families of 30, can use (limited) physical punishment and serve a different 'purpose' in their children's lives.

Standard of care

The standard of care you owe your pupils is that of a reasonably careful or prudent co-professional, that is, teacher in similar circumstances. The standard of care owed to pupils varies in different circumstances (for example, in the gym, science lab or regular classroom; in the school playground; on a field trip). Consider the factors listed by Mr Justice McIntyre (1981) as quoted by Roher and Wormwell (2002, pp. 45–6):

- the number of pupils being supervised at any given time
- the nature of the exercise or activity in progress
- the age of the pupil
- the degree of skill and training that the pupil may have received in connection with the activity
- the nature and condition of the equipment in use at the time
- the competence and capacity of the pupil involved.

> You have a duty to provide appropriate and reasonable supervision of pupils at the school. If you believe that particular circumstances exist at your school that prevent you from carrying out that duty, have an urgent discussion with your employer.

Duty to provide adequate supervision of pupils

1. *Ensure* that:

   (a) a supervision programme and a duty schedule are in place for all times when pupils are not in class
   (b) both regular and occasional staff know their duties
   (c) the supervision programme complies with collective agreements and local authority policies and procedures.

2. *Consider* specific supervision requirements.

   (a) Critical times:

      (i) in the school playground or building before and immediately after school
      (ii) at break time and lunch hour.

   (b) Critical areas:

      (i) in corridors and lunchrooms or cafeteria, in stairwells or on stairs
      (ii) at school gates.

(c) Special situations:

(i) school assemblies and social events, inclement weather, early dismissals

(ii) circumstances particular to your pupils, school, or community.

3. *Follow* the elements of a reasonable supervision policy:

(a) any applicable local authority policies and procedures
(b) supervision routines for particular activities or areas
(c) instructions to staff and pupils about expected conduct
(d) consideration of the ratio of staff to pupils for particular activities
(e) consideration of any inherent dangers;
(f) any special circumstances of individual pupils, individual special needs
(g) weather conditions for outdoor activities
(h) the geography of the area to be supervised (adapted from Batzel, quoted in Roher and Wormwell, 2002, p. 54).

4. *Conduct* a site safety audit at regular intervals.

(a) Take into consideration such factors as lines of sight when developing the supervision plan.
(b) Use your local authority's safety guidelines.

TIP

What will constitute adequate supervision of pupils?

Although headteachers have overall responsibility for the supervision of pupils, most direct supervision is provided by other employees, teachers and support staff. The headteacher's duty to supervise pupils is therefore often subsumed in the duty to supervise these other people. (*Note*: the headteacher's duty to supervise pupils also requires that adequate supervision, in terms of numbers, is in place.)

In addition to pupils, headteachers also have the following people under their professional supervision as regards the duty of care and to ensure that these people can go about their business in a supported manner: teachers, deputy and assistant headteachers, educational assistants and other on-site learning or behaviour staff, secretarial and administration staff, school visitors and volunteers.

TIP

Complying with relevant acts and regulations, following local authority policies and procedures, and exercising good judgement and common sense will all help to reduce significantly the risk of legal liability.

MAKE DECISIONS WISELY

- Take the time needed to make thoughtful decisions. Never make hasty decisions.
- Give yourself time to reflect and perhaps even sleep on it.
- Don't make a difficult decision today that can wait until tomorrow.
- Be sure to gather all the facts.
- Try to have a cooling-off period if you are under duress.
- Phone a colleague – just to be sure.
- Check with your professional association.
- Base your decision on common sense and how it will help children.

4 Management Skills

School leadership and management: an overview

As a headteacher, you exercise your leadership and management skills every day.

Leadership	Management	Administration
Doing the right things	Doing things right	Doing things
Path making	Path following	Path tidying
Complexity	Clarity	Consistency

(West-Burnham, 2004, p. 3)

The following are three skill sets that can enhance your effectiveness:

1. Time management
2. Delegation
3. Visibility.

Time management

> ### Successful time management
>
> - Enables you to gain a better perspective of pending activities and priorities.
> - Ensures more opportunities to be creative (being proactive rather than reactive).
> - Helps you deal with, reduce and often avoid stress.
> - Helps you gain more leisure time.
> - Enables you to attain your objectives consistently and systematically.
>
> (Jones, 2005, p. 55)

 Getting started

The biggest time management challenge is ensuring that you take control of your own time; it is possible to do this. Your other major challenge is identifying and focusing on what is important, rather than on 'busy' work.

Your desk – a good place to start

Your desk may be the best place to start your commitment to improved time management skills.

Your desk needs to be set up to meet your needs.

Committing to a clean desk policy and a well-organized workspace will help get you off to a good start.

Setting up your office

1. Maximize efficiency

Keep the files and materials that you use most frequently at your desk.
Programme the speed-dial numbers on your phone.
Organize your workspace for efficient accessibility.

2. Maximize personal safety and security

Plan for both open-door and closed-door meetings.
Install a window in solid doors.
Consider lines of sight, exits and other safety issues when configuring your office.
Set up procedures for office staff to monitor your meetings with difficult people.

3. Plan your office to convey the image and message you wish to project.

Display children's work.
Paperwork.
Take advice from secretariat about organizing your day.

⊙ Nine principles of time management: an overview

1. Establish priorities.
2. Welcome routines and procedures.
3. Transfer your 'monkeys' to someone else's back.
4. Delegate, delegate, delegate (see the 'Delegation' section of this chapter).
5. Manage incoming mail (including e-mails) and phone calls.
6. Organize your paperwork and your workspace.
7. Use time in large chunks when necessary.
8. Learn to say 'No', 'I don't know', 'No I can't', 'Not my job'.
9. Estimate your time needs.

Source: adapted from Crittendon, 2002, pp. 34–5.

> Your success comes down to the difference between managing your work and letting your work manage you.

Further reading

Covey, S., Merrill, A. and Merrill, R. (1999) *First Things First.*

TIPS Doing the right job at the right time:
more time management tips

1. *Plan*   – daily routine around important tasks.
2. *Review*   – 'to-do' list throughout the day.
              – tomorrow's agenda before you leave.
3. *Monitor* – time spent on low-priority items (which might be reading the mail, answering e-mails, talking on the phone).
              – time spent on the most important tasks.
4. *Don't*   – just react to events as they occur. Take a proactive approach to your day.
              – use routine interruptions (for example, the arrival of the mail) as an excuse to avoid important tasks.
              – ignore little problems; they may become big ones.
5. *Do*   – allow time for unexpected problems and essential interruptions.
              – allow more time than you think you'll need for each task.
              – set aside time by yourself or with others to work on major projects whenever necessary.

Do it, or delegate it. File it, or throw it out.

TIP

Delegation and distributed leadership

'The Strategic Challenge is to give work back to people without abandoning them. Overload them and they will avoid learning. Underload them and they will grow too dependent or complacent.'

(Heifetz, 1994, p. 251)

Delegation is important. You cannot do all the work yourself.

Decide what you are not going to do

'The headteacher's job is to ensure that essential things get done, not to do them all himself.'

(Fullan, 1997, p. 37)

Take care not to delegate too many tasks to just one or two willing and able people. Try to involve as many staff members as appropriate. Develop and practice distributed leadership.

Further reading

National College for School Leadership (2004) *Distributed Leadership*.

➔ Seven dimensions of delegation and related key behaviours of effective headteachers

1. Task identification

- Show confidence in yourself and be willing to let others assume authority.
- Identify tasks appropriate for staff and beneficial to the school.
- Retain responsibility for tasks functionally limited to the headteacher.
- Maintain the symbolic leadership role (for example, presenting important awards to pupils and staff).

2. Identification of delegatees

- Identify delegatees appropriate for the task or tasks. Consider the stage of career development of the delegatee.
- View delegation assignments as staff development opportunities as well as task accomplishment.
- Delegate tasks to the level nearest the action or concern (for example to teachers, deputy/assistant heads or support staff). Delegate to the lowest level that can achieve the results.

3. Authority and responsibility

- Delegate authority sufficient to accomplish the task.
- Be prepared to accept different approaches or different conclusions.
- Specify the limits of delegatee authority.
- Clarify delegatee accountability to the headteacher.

4. Support and feedback

- Make available necessary resources (for example, information, time, money, equipment, support services, facilities).
- Provide training if required.
- Maintain active interest and seek and give feedback.
- Make the school and community aware of the delegatees and their task(s).

5. Participation and autonomy

- Facilitate task accomplishment without interfering in the delegatees' work.
- Involve other individuals or groups in decisions as the work evolves.
- Maintain active communication with delegatees.

6. Accountability

- Plan the review and reporting process for the delegated task or project.
- Focus on results rather than process.
- Exhibit confidence in delegatees.
- Tailor the level of accountability to the experience of the delegatee and the significance of the task.

7. Evaluation

- Evaluate participant performance.
- Act on task results.
- Recognize accomplishments of individuals and groups.
- Organize closure activity as appropriate.

Source: the above dimensions are adapted from Thompson, 1993, pp. 7-10–7-15.

 Four delegation tips

1. Myths about delegation

- You cannot trust your employees to be responsible.
- When you delegate you lose control of a task and its outcome.

- You are the only one who has all the answers.
- You can do all the work faster by yourself.
- Delegation dilutes your authority.
- Your employees will be recognized for doing a good job, but you will not.
- Delegation decreases your flexibility.
- Your employees are too busy.
- Your staff do not see the big picture.

2. *The six steps of delegating*

- Communicate the task.
- Furnish context for the task.
- Determine standards.
- Grant authority.
- Provide support.
- Get commitment.

3. *Delegate these things*

- Detail work.
- Information gathering.
- Repetitive assignments.
- Surrogate roles (employees fill in for you at a meeting if appropriate).
- Future duties (to give employees a taste of their own future duties).

4. *Do not delegate these things*

- Don't only delegate chores.
- Long-term vision and goals.
- Performance appraisals, discipline and counselling.
- Politically sensitive situations.
- Personal assignments.
- Issues with confidential or sensitive circumstances.

> Be visible, do not delegate important symbolic tasks. You can, however, share these tasks.

Source: delegation tips adapted from Nelson and Economy, 1996.

Visibility: management by walking around

> While you are engaged in 'management by walking around', you have a perfect opportunity to 'walk your talk', to demonstrate through your words and actions the attitudes and behaviours that the school values. As the headteacher, you are a significant role model, and you will have a positive impact on the behaviour of others by visibly modelling desired behaviours yourself.

An overview

1. Practise planned visibility systematically so that pupils, teachers and the community know you care and are present.
2. Be visible in classrooms, in corridors, on the playground, in the cafeteria, at staff workshops, and so on.
3. Your presence at school events sends a message of concern and interest.
4. Visibility throughout the school day helps reduce pupil discipline problems, sets the school tone and promotes communication.
5. High visibility is a natural expression of concern and interest.

> Visibility – getting out of the office and being seen all over the school – was the most frequently identified quality of a strong school leader.

 Planned visibility: ten practical tips

Being visible promotes good communication. Positive, proactive communication can be a very enjoyable part of your school day, and it pays enormous dividends.

1. Get to know the names of staff members and of as many pupils as possible.
2. Walk the corridors before school in the morning.
3. Allow time for casual, informal encounters with staff members throughout the day.
4. Schedule times every day when you are in the corridors, playground, cafeteria, and so on.
5. Meet the school buses as they arrive, and greet the pupils, when possible.

6. Chat with parents as they drop pupils off in the morning or pick them up at night, when possible.
7. Visit the gym, library and school foyer whenever possible during the day; talk with pupils.
8. Go outside frequently during break times and the lunch hour.
9. Put yourself on the duty schedule; bus duty or early morning hall duty can work well.
10. Be highly visible. The more you are 'out and about', the more opportunities there are for positive, face-to-face communication. (If you are out of sight, you will be out of touch and out of mind.)

TIP

> A final word: be sure when you are 'out and about' in the school that you spend time in classrooms observing pupils and teachers at work. Classroom observation should be part of an *agreed* process with protocols, procedures, and so on.

DELEGATE

If you have not learned how to prioritize and delegate, do so quickly.
Offer those following you the leadership opportunities you were given. You cannot do it all yourself. Teamwork is the key.
Don't overload your willing horses.

5 Communication

Communication tips and checklists

Be visible

Positive, proactive communication can be a very enjoyable part of your school day, and it pays enormous dividends. Being visible promotes good communication. See 'Planned visibility: ten practical tips' in Chapter 4.

Practise active listening

One of the best ways you can establish yourself in your (new) school is to practise active listening. When you are building relationships, how well you listen is as important as what you say and how you say it. When you practise active listening, you make statements that encourage others to talk.

 Active listening techniques: six tips

1. *Encourage*

    (a) Draw the other person out.
    (b) Use verbal and non-verbal cues to show that you are really listening.
    (c) Convey attentiveness with body language and short vocal responses.
    (d) Be aware that appropriate body language and vocalizations vary from culture to culture.

    Examples: 'Can you tell me more?' and 'I'd like to hear about this'.

2. *Clarify*

    (a) Ask questions to confirm what the speaker has said.
    (b) Not only will this help you to understand, but it may also help the speaker examine his or her own perceptions.

    Examples: 'Could you tell me which of those things happened first?' and 'When did this happen?' 'Give me an example'.

3. *Restate*

    (a) Repeat in your words what the speaker has said.
    (b) This shows you are listening and helps check for facts and meaning.

    Examples: 'She told you she'd call right back and called two days later' and 'So you'd like your parent to trust you more, is that right?'

4. *Reflect*

    (a) In your own words, tell what you think the speaker is experiencing.
    (b) This can lead the speaker to be more expressive.
    (c) It also provides a way to check the accuracy of your perceptions.

    Examples: 'You seem quite upset' and 'It sounds like you felt angry'.

5.   *Summarize*

(a)   Reiterate the major ideas, themes and feelings that the speaker has expressed.
(b)   This provides review and a basis from which to continue the dialogue.

Examples: 'So the main problems you have with this are ...' and 'These seem to be the key ideas you've expressed'.

6.   *Validate*

(a)   Show appreciation for the speaker's efforts.
(b)   Acknowledge the value of talking.
(c)   Affirm your positive feelings about being part of the dialogue.

Examples: 'I'm really glad we're talking' and 'I appreciate your willingness to resolve this'.

> Don't just hear – listen.
> Listen constantly. Listen carefully. Listen thoughtfully.
> Listen and learn.

 Communication: ten basic tips

1.   Make communications a focus.
2.   Do not substitute technology for communication. Technology is an effective tool, not a substitute for good interpersonal communication.
3.   Consider who needs to know what, and how and when they will receive the information. Do not circulate information to a wide audience when only a few people will need to respond. 'Information overload' is an ever-present danger.
4.   Keep your communication as positive as possible. Avoid knee-jerk negative responses.
5.   If you are asked a question and you do not have the answer, respond with 'I don't know, but I'll find out', or maybe with 'I don't know, but I will ask (person X) to find out'.
6.   Be sensitive to misinterpretation of your writing. For example, written correspondence and e-mail that you may have written casually may be

taken very seriously by the recipient. Give each message a second reading. Read it from the recipient's perspective.

7. Don't fabricate excuses to cover your mistakes.
8. It's alright to change your mind when new evidence comes to light, as long as you don't do it so often that you are labelled indecisive.
9. Don't take yourself too seriously. (Take your work seriously, but not yourself.)
10. Once again, never underestimate the importance of communication, but make it clear to the audience why they are being told this and what they are to do with the information!

Source: Communication adapted from Crittendon, 2002, pp. 9–13.

Hierarchy of effective communication

Below are ten methods of communication, listed from most to least effective:

1. One-to-one or face-to-face communication
2. Small group discussions and meetings
3. Speaking before a large group
4. Telephone conversations
5. Handwritten personal notes
6. Typewritten, personal letters (not computer-generated letters)
7. Computer-generated 'personalized' letters
8. Brochures or pamphlets distributed by mail
9. Articles in organizational newsletters, magazines or tabloids
10. News releases carried in local newspapers.

School website

Your school website is a highly visible and very public form of communication.

- Keep protection of privacy in mind as you post items to the site.
- Check your local authority protocols.
- Be sure to assign responsibility for regular monitoring and updating of the school website.

✅ Who are your target audiences?

Always ask yourself: 'With *whom* should I communicate in this particular situation?' Consider pupils, staff, others at the school, parents, the school governing body, your local authority, other agencies, your professional associations, the community, and the media.

1. *Pupils*

   Pupils
   Pupils in the school council

2. *School-based staff*

   Administrative assistants and clerical staff
   Technicians
   Site staff (catering, cleaning, maintenance)
   Bursars
   Classroom assistants
   Library staff
   Supply teachers
   Occupational health and safety representative
   Teachers
   Union representatives
   Deputy and assistant heads
   School nurses and health staff

3. *Others associated with the school*

   Bus drivers
   Gap students and work-placement students
   Crossing patrols
   Evening lettings groups
   Site security personnel
   Outside catering staff
   Liaison officers from the local authority
   Staff of on-site child care (preschool, before- and after-school programmes) and other extended school activities
   Student teachers on teaching practice

4.   *Parents and guardians*

Carers/parents
Parent volunteers in the school

5.   *The governing body*

All governors
Community representatives, co-optees, associate governors
The chair of governors
Staff representatives on governing body
Pupil representatives (if any)
The clerk to the governors

6.   *Local authority and/or diocesan board*

Director of Children's Services
School improvement partner
Area educational psychologist or social worker assigned to your school
Administrative staff (for example, school transport)
Local authority councillors
Other headteachers in the district
Other schools in the neighbourhood
Education welfare officer

7.   *Other agencies*

Child and family services agencies
Local fire department
Local police force
Other community and social services
Probation services
Public health unit

8.   *Professional associations*

The teacher unions
School leader unions, for example National Association of Head Teachers
The support staff unions

National governors' associations
National parents' associations
Other government and national educational bodies – general teaching councils,
National College for School Leadership, and so on

9. The local community

Community members with children no longer in the school system
Community members without children
Households adjacent to the school
Local businesses
Local community groups (ethnic, cultural, religious, recreational)
Local government
Professional associations
Service clubs, Rotary, Prince's Trust, youth groups, and so on

10. Media

Local newspaper
Local radio
Local television
Local websites

Methods of communication

Always ask yourself: '*How* should I communicate in this particular situation?'

1. Written communication

Memos
Letters
E-mail
Daily or weekly bulletins for staff
Wall-size master calendar and individual copies
Notices posted on bulletin boards or whiteboard in staffroom or elsewhere
Information placed in individual staff mailboxes
Notices posted on school intranet for staff
Outdoor portable sign on lawn or roof for specific events (can be rented)

2. *Informal oral communication*

Passing conversations in hallway, school corridor, playground, but beware of misinterpretation after a hasty few words in passing
Brief one-to-one chats in office or classroom

3. *Meetings*

Scheduled one-to-one meetings
Staff meetings
Team meetings
Committee meetings
Large assemblies and pupil/parent evenings

4. *Formal oral communication*

Individual phone calls
Recorded messages on school phone
Computer programmed automated telephone dial-out messaging system
Morning announcements over the public address system

Written communication

Documents inventory: 20 forms of written communication

As a headteacher, your written communication takes many different forms, including those below:

1. *Agendas and minutes*: staff meetings, committee meetings
2. *Articles* for professional journals
3. *Funding proposals* and bids for grants
4. *General letters*: welcome to parents new to the school
5. *Newsletters*: staff newsletter, school newsletter
6. *Handbooks*: staff, pupil, parent
7. *Information brochures* and packages regarding school activities
8. *Letters of acknowledgement*
9. *Letters of recommendation*: staff, pupils, others
10. *Memos*: written reinforcement of verbal requests, general directions

11. *News releases* for local media (for further details see Chapter 6, 'Public and Media Relations')
12. *Proposals for presentations* in local or national conferences
13. *Reports*: staff performance management reports (confidential, of course)
14. *School plans*: professional development, school improvement, communication
15. *Special occasion cards*: get-well cards, birthday cards
16. *Summaries*: written summaries of consultation meetings, public meetings
17. *Surveys*: staff, pupil, parent, and community surveys
18. *Thank you notes* (handwritten) to staff, pupils, volunteers, others – very important and much appreciated
19. *Translations*: key parent communications translated into other languages
20. *Written responses* (if appropriate) to parent concerns and questions

> This list can serve as a memory jogger when you are selecting examples for your professional portfolio (see Chapter 29, 'Professional Learning and Personal Well-being').

TIP

Speaking versus writing

When should you give a message orally and when should you put it in writing?

1. Your choice will depend on:

   (a) how much time you have
   (b) how important the message is
   (c) the attitude and nature of your intended receiver(s)
   (d) whether you want to keep a permanent record.

2. You may want to send a message orally when:

   (a) you want immediate and direct feedback
   (b) you don't want a written record (if writing will commit you too firmly to a course of action and take away your options or flexibility)
   (c) there is not enough time to put something in writing
   (d) delivering the message in person will increase its impact or urgency.

3. You may want to write a message when:

    (a) several people must act on the same instructions
    (b) there are regulatory, legal, or contractual requirements involved
    (c) you want to take a formal position on the matter, clarify an opinion, or dispel a rumour
    (d) you want to provide a precise set of instructions
    (e) the receiver tends to disregard or forget oral instructions.

Source: adapted from Straub, 2000, pp. 150–1.

Document, document, document

Document all important meetings, conversations, telephone calls and incidents that have any future possibility of concern, contention or controversy. If there is likely to be a dispute then provide the other party with a copy of the document, signed and dated, with a list of those to whom it is being circulated. The document should list all decisions, reasons and action points, and by whom.

 Reasons for putting it in writing

1.   To refresh your memory.
2.   To allow time to reread, absorb, and consider facts and ideas.
3.   To document occurrences, behaviours, meetings.
4.   To ensure accuracy of records; to keep lists of facts, dates, figures.
5.   To give or receive orders or instructions.
6.   To prepare reports (for example, accident reports).
7.   To prevent misunderstandings.
8.   To save time; to plan ahead; to organize.
9.   To state or to confirm an agreement.
10.   To keep track of what has been said (Fritz, 2001, p. 240).

Unless there is a specific reason to put a communication in writing, don't.

1.   Give priority to face-to-face communication.
2.   Communication by phone should generally be your second choice, after face-to-face communication.

3. If your local authority or governing body has a form for documenting particular circumstances, use it.
4. Do document all your significant meetings, whether in person or by phone.
5. When you send any written communication to someone, consider whether e-mail or hard copy is more appropriate.
6. When you do put something contentious or significant in writing, edit, rewrite and reread it again (at a later time if possible) before sending it.
7. Time is almost always on your side, so don't rush important written communication.
8. Many things that you write can be used for several purposes, with little or no modification. This can be a great time saver. For example, a brief overview of a subject curriculum can be used in the school newsletter, as an introduction to the course outline, and as a handout at a curriculum evening or governing body group presentation.
9. Save electronic copies (and hard copies where appropriate) of letters, reports, newsletters, and so on, and use them as templates in the future.
10. Use the sample letters created by your employer (for example, for exclusions).

 Tips for communicating by e-mail

Tone

- Avoid jokes or sarcasm; what you find funny may be obnoxious or offensive to others.
- Be careful about your message's tone; it is easy for someone to misinterpret it.
- If your message is very important, controversial or confidential, or could be easily misunderstood, use the telephone or set up a face-to-face meeting.
- Send positive messages so recipients will look forward to receiving them.
- To communicate a negative message, pick up the phone or, even better, schedule a face-to-face meeting.
- When writing e-mail messages, use the same diction and common sense you would use if you were writing a letter, talking on the phone or meeting face-to-face.

Format

- Create a signature file to automatically appear at the bottom of each of your messages: your name, title, school, address and e-mail address, and phone number.
- Keep the message short and simple.
- Put the most important information in the first line of the first paragraph.
- When you send or receive an e-mail message that contains important information, save a copy on your hard drive and/or print out a copy and file it.
- Write a subject line that is descriptive (for example, 'attend Tues. meeting at 9.30').
- Write messages that are easy to respond to; readers can reply *yes* or *no*.

Audience

- If it is not necessary to respond to each and every e-mail message, don't.
- Don't send copies to people who don't need to see your message.
- Double check that you are e-mailing just those who you wish to receive it.

Etiquette

- Always reread your e-mail message before sending it.
- Beware of crying wolf; use the *Urgent Message* notation sparingly.
- Don't write e-mail messages using all capital letters: it is known as shouting.
- Remember: e-mail messages are not private. Never write anything in an e-mail message that you would not want to become public.
- Run your spell-checker and proofread your message.
- The fewer messages you send, the greater the attention they will receive.

Note: You may not want to start active e-mail correspondence with hundreds of parents; it can be overwhelming. However, e-mail is a great way to communicate with staff members.

TIP

Know the difference between *Reply Sender* and *Reply All*. Be careful every time.

School newsletters

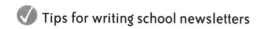 Tips for writing school newsletters

1. Check your local authority recommendations with respect to use of pupils' names and photos.

2. Adopt a catchy name and logo and a readily identified masthead.

3. Use bold attention-getting headlines.

4. Adopt a right-to-the-point writing style.

5. Share your personal priorities as the school leader.

6. Insert clip-and-save calendars.

7. When reproducing materials, don't break copyright laws.

8. Include lots of pupil quotes, pupil writing, and examples of pupil work.

9. Include photos and reproductions of pupil artwork.

10. Leave plenty of white space.

11. Include items that reinforce school curriculum and learning.

12. Publish regularly.

13. Consider publishing your newsletter by e-mail or on the school home page if your community is online.

14. Use response sheets to generate feedback and two-way communication; seek feedback. (To encourage response, put returns into a draw for a prize.)

15. Proofread, proofread, proofread.

16. Try to avoid jargon and acronyms, running too long (consider a one-pager with calendar on reverse), talking down to readers.

Note: Be sure to have appropriate prior permission before including childrens' names, photos, work samples, and so on in your newsletter.

If you publish your newsletter electronically or post it on your school website, extra care is required regarding the inclusion of photos of pupils or pupils' names.

The effectiveness of school newsletters

Parents learn about their children's schools through many sources:

1. Conversations with their children
2. Their children's reports
3. The school newsletter
4. Parent–teacher meetings
5. Personal visits to the school
6. Teacher notes and phone calls
7. Conversations with friends and neighbours
8. Parent–teacher evenings
9. Open houses at the school, consultation evenings
10. Local newspapers

✅ Distribution of school newsletters

Arrange with several headteachers to send school newsletters to each other every month. Develop a distribution list for your school newsletter that includes:

1. Parents

2. Staff

3. Local authority staff who visit your school regularly (for example, education welfare officers, education psychologists)

4. Bus drivers

5. Director of Children's Services

6. Governing body

7. Community businesses or organizations

8. Other schools in your area

9. Day care or other providers operating in the school

10. Local politicians

School communication plan

Develop a school communication plan.

1. In every situation you face, consider these five key questions:

    (a) *What* information do you want to communicate?
    (b) *Why* do you want to communicate the information?
    (c) *Who* needs to receive the information?
    (d) *How* should the information be communicated?
    (e) *When* should the information be communicated?

2. When developing your school communication plan, ask the following six questions:

    (a) Who is my audience?
    (b) What is my key message?
    (c) What strategy/vehicle will be successful?
    (d) Who is responsible?
    (e) What are the timelines?
    (f) How will I measure success?

Your communication plan might follow a format similar to the one below.

Audience	Key Messages	Strategies	Person Responsible	Timelines

For more information on developing a school communication plan see 'Developing a public relations strategy for your school' in Chapter 6.

Also, see Chapter 9, 'Records and Information Management', for further information regarding confidentiality and communication, and Chapter 26, 'Emergency Preparedness', for further information regarding crisis communication.

COMMUNICATE CONSTANTLY

Remember:　As the school leader, there are certain things that are not appropriate for you to say.

Build strong relationships with parents and the community; the rewards for the pupils and the school are endless.

Appreciate the value of listening. Colleagues, parents and pupils all need to feel they have been heard before they feel ready to listen.

Practise active listening.

6 Public and Media Relations

Developing a public relations strategy for your school

Public relations

Headteachers need to be able to change negative attitudes and build on positive ones to develop public support for education in general and schools in particular.

This support must be earned on an ongoing basis throughout the school year.

Public relations is the vehicle through which this occurs.

'A good public relations plan centres on communicating, educating and influencing your school community.'

(Thompson, 1993, pp. 21–3)

1. When developing your school's public relations strategy, keep in mind that such plans:

   (a) require a community focus
   (b) are low-cost and practical
   (c) require that parents play a key role in relationships with the school
   (d) recognize staff communication as the starting point for all public relations activities
   (e) manage crises to limit damage to the school's reputation
   (f) require that headteachers work effectively with the media
   (g) utilize technology to improve their effectiveness (Thompson, 1993, pp. 21–5).

> **Remember**
>
> 1. Effective public relations strategies begin with effective staff communication.
> 2. Always communicate internally (with your entire staff) before communicating externally.

2. Before building your school's public relations plan, you need to be aware of your local authority's communication and public relations protocols. Check your local authority's policies and procedures regarding public relations and communications. Find out who the press and public relations officers are in your local authority. Determine their responsibilities:

   (a) Do they write news releases?
   (b) Are they the media spokespersons for your school?
   (c) Can you talk to the media yourself?
   (d) How do they promote individual school stories?
   (e) Do they need to see and sign off materials such as press releases before the materials are released to the media?

Arrange to meet with your local authority public relations officer to establish a personal connection. If your school is not a community school, you may nevertheless contact the press and public relations department to see if they can advise on media contact. Your diocese may also be able to advise.

3. Be sure your school communication plan identifies ways to:

   (a) provide complete, accurate information to staff in a timely manner
   (b) obtain feedback from staff and establish effective two-way communication
   (c) seek the advice and input of staff right from the start, as you design your school's public relations strategy.

4. When building your school's public relations plan, seek feedback from the parents as well. You might use:

   (a) a suggestion box in the school foyer or library
   (b) a reply sheet in the newsletter
   (c) a dedicated voice mailbox
   (d) your school website
   (e) brief questionnaires or surveys.

5. Communication plans and public relations programmes must provide many opportunities:

   (a) to listen
   (b) to receive as well as send information
   (c) to promote two-way communication.

6. Feed stories to the local media, in the good times. Then, if and when the bad times come, the local media may be fairer to you.
7. Remember that often modest or trivial stories can make good copy – journalists need stories.
8. Always be ready with a quote; offer an alternative view to a journalist – they thrive on differing opinions.
9. The media exist to sell papers or media time; don't expect them to be 'nice' or 'fair' to you.

TIPS Tips for writing a press release

1. Make sure your story is newsworthy. (Ask yourself: 'Would I be interested in this if I were not a headteacher?')
2. Keep it short and punchy to grab attention. Limit your news release to one page, if possible. Consider adding a fact sheet as supplementary information.

3. Summarize the most important facts about the story – the who, what, where, when and why – in your lead paragraph.
4. Use a catchy headline to summarize your story and capture the recipient's attention.
5. Include quotes; reporters will often take a quote directly from the release, so providing some helps get your message out in your own words.
6. Ensure the information is timely. All media outlets are bound by deadlines. Find out what the deadlines are, and be strategic in releasing your information.
7. Always put a date on your release.
8. Check the accuracy of your information. Double-check your facts and figures, and attribute third-party information to a legitimate source.
9. Make sure the information is easy to read and to understand – avoid education jargon and acronyms.
10. Include a contact person and phone number in case journalists need additional information.
11. Target your efforts. Take time to find out who covers education and direct your material to that specific individual. (Keep your media lists current; media people tend to move around a lot.)
12. Watch your spelling and grammar: check for typos.

 ## Tips for giving media interviews

Before the interview

When approached by the media to give an interview, collect the following information:

1. What is the name, phone number and fax number of the reporter?
2. What is the name of the media outlet?
3. What is the subject of the interview?
4. What is the specific angle?
5. What is the reporter's real deadline?
6. How long will the interview last and where will it be conducted? (This will need to be negotiated.)
7. Who else will the reporter be talking to?
8. Can you provide them with some background information in advance?

9. What kind of story is this feature – business, social, political?
10. Ask the question: 'is there anything else you can tell me about this?'

Give yourself time to prepare for the interview:

1. Talk to others in the school if they are involved in the issue.
2. Prepare for the toughest questions.
3. Practise and rehearse.

During the interview

1. Do not answer questions when:

   (a) the local authority, governors, school staff or parents are not yet informed about the issue
   (b) pupil privacy is involved
   (c) there is a disaster or emergency – you must notify family first
   (d) there is a news blackout
   (e) the issue is before the courts.

2. Pause before answering each question:

   (a) Take time to collect your thoughts.
   (b) Decide whether you want to answer this question. (Does it deal directly with you or your school?)
   (c) Determine whether there is a way you can use your key messages to answer this question.
   (d) Consider a reply using your own words, not those of the reporter.

Key messages

What do people remember?
What do they tell others?
What appears in the story?

3. Use key messages:

   (a) You need to create a balance between the reporter's goal (to get the information needed to prepare a story) and your goal (to represent your school and get your key messages out).
   (b) Prepare three key messages.
   (c) Use simple words.
   (d) Have an interesting, different, unique point of view.
   (e) Use catchy phrases or words (if appropriate).
   (f) Support key messages with clear, concise examples.
   (g) Insert your key messages into the interview; don't push them.

> Send a personalized thank you note to the reporter when your school is highlighted.

Media interviews

Do

1. Prepare key messages in advance; know your story; practice.
2. Treat each interview as special, as an opportunity.
3. Respect a reporter's deadline.
4. Be responsive; be honest; be yourself.
5. Stay calm.
6. Stick to your messages and keep it simple.
7. Stick to the agreed-on time and location.
8. Provide additional background information.
9. Leave your business card.
10. Mention the name of your school if it is a good news story.

Don't

1. Use jargon or acronyms.
2. Guess, speculate, or comment on rumours.
3. Answer hypothetical questions.
4. Say 'no comment'.

5. Speak 'off the record'.
6. Let a reporter put words in your mouth.
7. Speak on behalf of others.
8. Express a personal view.

CREATE A POSITIVE FIRST IMPRESSION
You only have one chance to make a first impression; make the most of it.

7 Managing Conflict and Difficult People

Introduction

People who complain about you

People who complain about you may do so for various reasons:

- You may have made a mistake or an error of professional judgement.
- They may not like you or may not agree with your management approach.
- You, as headteacher are seen as the embodiment of 'authority' – it is not a personal complaint.
- The complainant is deluded, deranged or destructive.
- Staff may oppose your management style or direction.
- Parents may accuse you of failing to deal with their children or other children to their satisfaction.
- Individual governors may intrude on your right to manage and lead, misunderstanding their corporate role in governance.

In your dealings with staff, remember that you have the authority of your governing body to manage the school as you see fit within the broad boundary of reasonableness.

If you are accused of unreasonable professional behaviour, the accuser would have to show that no other headteacher would be expected to behave in this fashion – quite a demanding level of proof.

When dealing with teachers, the School Teachers' Pay and Conditions Document Part 12 says 'a teacher … shall carry out the professional duties of a teacher as circumstances may require, under the reasonable direction of the headteacher'. So, for a complaint that a headteacher was making unreasonable demands to be a valid complaint, the teacher would have to show to the governing body that the headteacher's requirement was:

(a) not a professional duty of a teacher, or
(b) circumstances did not require it, or
(c) the direction is unreasonable.

For non-teaching staff the same principles would apply.

It is very rare for a governing body to rule against a headteacher unless the headteacher has behaved in a quite unreasonable manner.

People who complain about each other and people who do not behave properly

Before a complainant resorts to an official procedure to progress their complaint against another person, or before you have to implement an official procedure to enforce compliance by an uncooperative individual, it will usually be necessary to deal with the complaint or conflict on a face-to-face, informal basis.

Some conflict arises indirectly, with people whispering in corners or there being an 'atmosphere' – always difficult to pin down.

Consider first how you, and others, react to conflict, what style of response you have to a conflict, and what mechanisms exist within informal and ultimately formal procedures.

Reacting to conflict

Reaction to conflict falls into three basic categories:

1. avoidance
2. problem-solving
3. confrontation.

When dealing with conflict, it can be helpful to notice how the parties are reacting to the situation, whether it is pupils, staff, parents or others. It is useful to monitor your own reaction to conflict in a variety of circumstances. A problem-solving approach has the best results.

The chart below can be used as an informal checklist to gauge your own or others' reactions to a situation of conflict.

Avoidance has a tendency to	Problem-solving has a tendency to	Confrontation has a tendency to
• allow self to be interrupted, subordinated, stereotyped	• state feelings, needs and wants directly	• interrupt, subordinate and stereotype others
• have poor eye contact	• have good eye contact	• have intense and glaring eye contact
• have poor posture and defeated air	• have straight posture and competent air	• have invading posture and arrogant air
• withhold information, opinions and feelings	• be able to disclose information, opinions and feelings	• conceal information, opinions and feelings
• be an ineffective listener	• be an effective listener	• be an ineffective listener
• be indecisive	• initiate and take clear positions	• dominate
• apologize, avoid and leave	• approach with skill	• be loud, abusive, blaming and sarcastic

Consider next what mechanisms exist to resolve a conflict without resorting to an official procedure.

Conflict resolution: an overview

Principles of conflict resolution

1. Look for solutions ... not for blame.
2. Focus on the problem ... not on the person.
3. Take a non-adversarial approach ... not an adversarial approach.
4. Use dialogue ... not debate.
5. Focus on interest ... not on position.
6. Try for a win/win solution ... not a win/lose one.
7. Focus on change ... not on control.

If the conflict is between two members of your school community, then there are a number of techniques to be used before the two parties go to an official dispute process.

Conflict resolution: a continuum

Approaches to conflict resolution range from negotiation, to conciliation, to mediation, to arbitration, to litigation.

	Unofficial approach		Official procedures		
	Negotiation	*Conciliation*	*Mediation*	*Arbitration*	*Litigation*
Disputants **speak to**	each other	each other	mediator/ each other	arbitrator	lawyer/ judge
Decision is **made by**	disputants	disputants	disputants	arbitrator	judge

In the school setting: negotiation may be an agreement to solve the problem, conciliation may be an agreement to settle differences as far as possible and to move forward, and mediation may involve a third party to offer shuttle diplomacy, to establish positions and look to common ground.

If these approaches fail, then official procedures commence. Arbitration will mean a senior person, for example, the headteacher, will review both sides of the conflict, and decide in one person's favour. There may be a right of appeal say, to the governing body. Litigation, where an aggrieved person takes their opponent to court for damages or redress, will be rare. A court would expect all school internal procedures to have been concluded.

How to use mediation

As headteachers may have to arbitrate while following an official procedure, it may be helpful for the previous stage of mediation to be attempted using some other mediator.

Do proceed to suggest mediation if:

1. the conflict is specific
2. both parties perceive the mediator to be neutral
3. both parties have voluntarily agreed to try mediation
4. not dealing with the conflict is unacceptable to both disputants
5. adequate time and space are available.

Do not suggest mediation if:

1. the matter includes police involvement or any legal ramifications
2. the case involves any form of harassment
3. the matter is the subject of a formal union grievance
4. the two sides are manifestly unequal
5. you are in doubt about the availability or capability of the mediator.

There are some commonsense points to be made when dealing with a complaint, either against oneself or between two people.

 Mediation and negotiation: ten tips

1. Separate the people from the problem.
2. Focus attention on interests, not positions.
3. Invent alternative options for mutual gain.
4. Base outcomes on objective standards and criteria.
5. Never yield to pressure, only to principle.
6. Don't attack positions; look behind them.
7. Don't defend ideas; ask for criticism and improvements.

8. In the face of personal attacks, rephrase the problem.
9. Ask questions.
10. Use silence.

Dealing with difficult people and complaints

TIPS *Tips on handling complaints*

Pay attention	Take all complaints seriously. Don't let small concerns become big ones.
Document	Document each complaint. Record the time and date of the call or meeting, and make notes of what was said. File your documentation.
Listen	Practise active listening. Rephrase what you have heard to verify understanding. Ask for further clarification if needed.
	Try to determine if there are underlying issues involved, or just the specific incident that is being reported. Listen to the complainant's feelings and ideas.
	See Chapter 5, 'Communication', for further tips regarding active listening.
Investigate	Get all the facts from the complainant.
	Check out the facts with all parties involved before responding.
Respond	An initial response is important, at least to acknowledge the complaint. Promise to look into the matter and reply to the complainant at a specified time.
	Don't make hasty promises that you cannot keep.
	Consider referring the complaint to another relevant member of staff if they are involved in the issue, but only if you have confidence in their ability to deal with the complaint.
Avoid	Avoid becoming defensive. Don't fabricate excuses.
	Avoid the use of inappropriate language, even if the complainant uses such language. If nothing else, agree to disagree. Remain polite and professional; stay calm.
	If the complainant becomes abusive and does not respond to your appeal for reason, discontinue the meeting or the phone call.

Relationships with Parents

There are some particular issues when dealing with parents.

 Dealing with problem parents

1. *Communicate*
    Deal with the issue as soon as is reasonably possible.
    Communicating in a consistent and efficient manner allows the parent to feel that concerns are addressed meaningfully.
    Listen for both the immediate concern and for underlying issues.

2. *Consider*
Possible references to consult include:

- the school's code of conduct and pupil disciplinary codes
- school handbook advice on organizational matters
- governing body policies and procedures.

3. *Respond*
Occasionally, parents become confrontational and hostile when they believe that their issue or complaint or child is not being dealt with appropriately. There are a number of strategies and ultimately legal tools that may be used to deal with the problem of parental harassment. The difficulty is determining when such tactics are necessary and which tactic is appropriate in the circumstances.

TIPS

If you feel you are dealing with a problem parent

- Alert your chair of governors.
- Call your professional association.
- Keep your local authority informed.
- Ultimately, if the parent is hostile or refuses to accept a negotiated way forward with the headteacher, then the official complaints procedure will need to be invoked, with a final stage of referral to a governing body panel for an ultimate verdict.

Issues and advice regarding relationships with parents

1. Issue
What should a headteacher do when confronted with a parent who is being physically violent or threatening violence against him or her?

Advice
Terminate the interview, use school security staff or procedures to remove the parent.
Contact the police to inform them of the threat.
Restrict the parent's access to the school in accordance with your governing body's policies or ask the local authority to withdraw the parent's right to enter the school's premises.

2. Issue
What should a headteacher do when a parent disrupts the school by persistently coming onto school property to confront staff or fails to behave reasonably on site, not registering at reception, entering inappropriate areas, or undermining school discipline and organization?

Advice
Advise the parent of the protocols of being a visitor.
Insist on the parent behaving reasonably on site, confirming by letter.
Implement a banning order through the local authority if the parent persists in behaving unacceptably.

> **Relationships with parents: an ounce of prevention is worth a pound of cure**
> Be proactive.
> Encourage healthy sharing of opinions and constructive criticism.
> Recognize the warning signs of potential problems.
> Highlight expectations for parent conduct with particular reference to the purpose of the code of conduct.

TAKE CARE TO COMMUNICATE EFFECTIVELY WITH PARENTS

The one thing that seems to keep things running smoothly is information to parents in a timely fashion. Even if the news is not good, parents and guardians need to hear it.

Learn how to have positive and effective communication with parents. Dealing with parents is without doubt one of the most stressful parts of the job.

Fight the urge to interrupt angry parents when they say something that is not true or not grounded. Be patient; wait and listen before you start correcting or setting the facts straight. Even if the parents still disagree with you, they feel like you have listened.

Relationships with governors

Governors have a role as members of a corporate body, making recommendations and taking decisions in a properly constituted committee, preferably following a resolution, properly worded, proposed and seconded, and voted upon.

Outside a committee, individual governors have no power to require that their views are adopted; they should not be involved with or aware of any cases that the headteacher is dealing with. A 'case' is an individual situation involving a pupil, member of staff or family that is confidential and is an operational, personnel or organizational issue.

The chair of governors has no extra power except in an emergency when (rarely) a chair has to take executive action to avoid serious imminent damage to the school.

Any complaints between governors should be dealt with by the chair advised by the clerk.

Any complaints by the governors about the action of headteacher or a member of staff should follow the complaints procedure for parents.

Relationships with staff

If your efforts to encourage staff to behave properly or to follow instructions are unsuccessful on an unofficial basis, then you will have to move to:

1. a misconduct procedure, if they refuse a legitimate instruction
2. a capability procedure, if they are incapable of following a legitimate instruction.

Informal means outside an official procedure, thus any informal meetings/discussions will have no official status or binding commitment.

Formal means within an agreed official procedure adopted by the governing body – thus any meetings/decisions/actions will have status, form part of a 'case' record and make enforceable commitments.

Before any official procedure commences it is important to make clear to the member of staff, at an earlier management meeting, the:

1. standards of performance or behaviour required
2. evidence that the member of staff is failing significantly to meet those standards
3. requirements that those standards are to be met, and the timescale for adherence.

Obviously this comment does not apply if the conduct is criminal or gross professional misconduct, that is, theft, assault, and so on.

It is quite proper for a headteacher to require staff to display a professional style and demeanour, as well as to deliver satisfactory outcomes and perform duties at a satisfactory standard.

Extremely provocative, temperamental, unsupportive, destructive, challenging or perverse behaviour or attitude can and must be challenged by headteachers.

8 Effective Meetings

Meetings may be part of an official procedure, for example, performance management reviews, child protection strategy meetings, governors meetings, disciplinary hearings, or they may be routine school management meetings, meetings with parents, staff meetings, Senior Leadership Team meetings or working groups. Prepare thoroughly for every meeting that you chair. To run effective meetings consider what must be done:

1. before the meeting (planning)
2. during the meeting (conducting)
3. after the meeting (following up).

Before the meeting

1. Consider four key questions

- Who has called the meeting?
- What is the objective of the meeting?
- Do we really need to have this meeting?
- What are the expected outcomes?

If you have called the meeting and it is needed, start planning. If you are called to a meeting which has clear objectives and a realistic set of expected outcomes, do what you can to ensure the planning is thorough.

2. Plan the agenda

- Consult the 'meeting planning checklist' below.
- Notify participants well in advance of the time, location, and purpose of the meeting.
- Consult with participants for agenda items.
- Agree with participants what documentation should be studied before the meeting, and what documentation should be brought to the meeting.
- Carefully consider the order in which you place the items.
- Consider whether purely informative items can be communicated by memo or e-mail instead.
- Distribute the agenda in advance of the meeting.
- Ensure that meeting dates and format conform to agreed procedures.

3. Do your homework

- Collect and organize reference materials for the meeting.
- Prepare handouts and audiovisual presentations (for example, PowerPoint).
- Before the meeting, speak with any individuals who have a vested interest in any agenda items. (For example, teachers should not hear about changes to their teaching assignments for the first time in a full staff meeting.)
- Alert individuals who are required to speak to an item on the agenda.

4. The status of the meeting

Is it part of a formal personnel procedure or other formal process which is laid down in the governing body's policies and procedures, for example, disciplinary, appraisal, child protection, governors committee, redundancy review, and so on? If so, the meeting procedure will be carefully detailed and should be followed. The decisions made at the conclusion of the meeting are likely to be (a) enforceable and (b) lead to significant actions or decisions.

If the meeting is not part of a formal procedure, nevertheless it may well be important and significant.

It will be vital to make clear to the participants whether the meeting is

- for information giving only: a watching brief
- for consultation with the attendees: with a final decision being made by the headteacher or senior team at a later date
- for negotiation with the attendees: seeking a mutually agreeable solution from all participants.

So often attendees are disappointed if their views articulated at a meeting are not acted upon: the clarity above is essential to avoid raising false expectations.

The phrases 'formal' and 'informal' are capable of alternative interpretations.

However, formal meetings are normally those held as part of an agreed procedure: conclusions are likely to be binding. Informal meetings are those where no binding decisions are made.

Meeting planning checklist

1. *Meeting*	Date
	Starting time
	Ending time
	Location
2. *Participants*	Number of participants
	List of participants' names
	Name cards for tables
3. *Facilities*	Accessibility for persons with disabilities
	Appropriate room size
	Adequate lighting/heating/cooling/ventilation
	Seating: chevron
	U-shaped
	classroom
	round table
	cabaret
	open circle or square
	extra chairs for guests
	tables for participants to write on
	Signs directing guests to meeting room
4. *Refreshments*	Tea, coffee, juice, bottled water
	Snack food: biscuits, fruit
5. *Equipment*	Laptop computer
	Overhead projector
	Data projector
	Slide projector

	Television and DVD player	
	Whiteboard	
6. *Supplies*	Extension cords	
	Extra bulbs	
	Extra copies of the agenda and previous minutes	
	Flip charts	
	Handouts	
	Markers	
	Masking tape	
	Overhead pens	
	Paper and pens	
	Transparencies	

Sample meeting agendas

1. Governing body meeting agenda

* Welcome and introductions
* Apologies
* Minutes of previous meeting
* Matters arising
* Headteacher's report
* Reports from other committees
* Other business as per agenda
* Any other business (AOB)/items for next agenda
* Date, time, place of next meeting

2. Agenda for brief or informal meetings

When	Meeting date	
	Starting time	
	Ending time	
Where	Location	
Why	Purpose of meeting	
Who	Person who called meeting	
	Names of meeting participants	
What	Agenda items	Time allocated
	1. _____	_____ minutes
	2. _____	_____ minutes
	3. _____	_____ minutes

Stand-up meetings

For very brief meetings, consider calling a 'stand-up' staff meeting. A stand-up meeting saves time settling in. It clearly signals that the meeting is designed to pass along information, not to engage in discussion or decision-making.

Wait until everyone has assembled before making announcements. Some schools have five minute briefings at the start of each day.

3. Staff meetings: two sample agendas

Sample No. 1 Staff meeting agenda
Monday, 24 February 2003
4.00 p.m. – 5.00 p.m.
Library

Refreshments

1. Welcome and introductions (new staff and student teachers)
2. Guest speaker: citizenship education: local authority PHSE coordinator
3. Debriefing regarding Fire Drill on 20 February
4. Staff training regarding mid-year summative assessments
5. Administrative matters (5 minutes)

TIP

Some headteachers find it helpful to divide staff meeting agendas items into three categories:

For decision   For discussion   For information

Items can then be placed in order of priority on the agenda and time allocated accordingly.

Sample No. 2 Staff meeting agenda
Tuesday, 25 March 2003
4.00 p.m. – 5.00 p.m.
Staffroom

Coffee and doughnuts available starting at 3.45 p.m.

1. Welcome and introductory remarks
2. Information items and announcements (see items posted on staff intranet)

3. Items for discussion and decision
4. Professional development:
   The Written Curriculum, the Taught Curriculum, and the Tested Curriculum: a presentation by staff members who attended the recent conference
5. Committee reports:
   Staff governors' report
   Information and Communication Technology Committee
6. Items of new business (added here at start of meeting; to be discussed or deferred to next meeting)
7. Dates to note: see attached calendar for April
8. Meeting ends: 5.00 p.m.

Next full-staff meeting: Tuesday, 11 May, 4.00 p.m. – 5.00 p.m.

During the meeting

Before the meeting starts, check that the equipment is working. If the group meets regularly, establish a meeting schedule for the year. Otherwise, set the next meeting date at the end of each meeting.

 How to run effective meetings: tips for the chair

Opening

Start and end the meeting on time.
Keep opening remarks welcoming but brief.
Introduce any guests.
Review the agenda. Keep to the agenda and the timelines.

Conducting
  If new business items are raised and there is not time for them, note them and carry them forward to the next meeting.
  Maintain order and focus. Discuss one piece of business at a time.
  Do not allow discussions that breach privacy or are discussions of a confidential individual case.

Participating
  Allow for individual and small-group input during discussion items. Try to involve all participants.

Remain neutral and provide alternative ways to solve problems or make decisions.

Encourage decision-making through consensus.

Formalize decisions through rules of order, if desired.

Closing

Summarize the meeting, reviewing key actions and decisions.

Check that all participants have the same understanding of any decisions.

Review the time, date and location of the next meeting and any items of new business that will be included on the next agenda.

Ensure that the meeting room is cleaned and restored to its original condition.

> **Establishing norms for the meeting**
>
> At the beginning of the meeting, use consensus to establish the norms of the meeting.
>
> This may not be necessary every time you meet if you have a regular group of participants who clearly understand and agree upon the norms for the meeting.
>
> However, if it is the first time the group has met, if the circumstances have changed, or if the group has new members or observers, take time at the beginning of the meeting to establish the norms for behaving and decision-making.

After the meeting

Ensure that minutes are written and distributed to all participants and to those members who were unable to attend. The minutes should be clear as to ACTIONS and BY WHOM.

Keep commitments you made during the meeting to take certain actions or to find particular information and pass it along.

Send thank you notes to those who made a presentation or an extra contribution toward the success of the meeting.

Begin the process of planning for the next meeting.

From time to time, seek input from group members regarding the effectiveness of the meetings. Ask for suggestions for improvement and implement those that are feasible.

⊙ Meetings at a distance: using technology to save time and money

Some meetings can be held successfully at a distance, using any one of three different approaches: audio conference calls, video conferencing, or web conferencing.

Meetings at a distance save participants the time and expense of travelling to a meeting site.

Once a face-to-face relationship has been established among participants, electronic meetings can be quite effective.

Start by asking yourself two questions:

1. What is the objective of the meeting?
2. Do we really need to have this meeting?

To have a successful meeting at distance, you must follow all the traditional steps for planning an effective meeting.

Meeting correspondence (notice of meetings, agenda, minutes) can be handled electronically.

Consider carefully the purpose of your meeting before deciding to meet at a distance rather than in person.

KEEP YOUR SENSE OF HUMOUR

Have a sense of humour. Laugh a lot, especially at yourself. Do not take anything too personally; it is not about you.

9 Records and Information Management

Getting started

Two administrative duties you must become familiar with are those concerning pupil records, financial records and other records, and secondly, school information management. *Records* include information about pupils and required reports that are kept at the school. *Information management* involves the organization of both paper and electronic files.

1. *When you review the management of pupil, financial and other records* ensure that you have appropriate security and backup systems in place to preserve and protect the privacy of all your electronic records. The local authority may require that a paper copy be filed of records that were generated electronically (for example, letters of exclusion, suspension, and so on).

2. *When you organize your own office,* follow the existing filing practices at first; take time to determine whether there is any need to alter these procedures at some point in the future. Some headteachers have filing cabinets in their offices; others ask their administrative assistants to keep all paper files in the general office. Ask the school secretary and deputy headteacher to brief you regarding existing procedures used for record and information management. Follow your local authority procedures for information management.

3. *When you store information,* you must do so in such a way that it can easily be accessed when needed; at the same time, access must be restricted to those who have a right to the information. Maintaining confidentiality of information is the responsibility of every staff member. Ensure that everyone at the school, including visiting staff, student teachers, and volunteers, handles all personal information with discretion. Freedom of information and data protection are outlined in legislation. Follow your local authority procedures regarding how to establish, maintain, retain, transfer and dispose of pupil records.

If records and information management is a priority for you for this year, arrange to visit experienced colleagues at other schools to discuss their procedures.
Also arrange for your school secretary to do the same.

TIP

Copying

Familiarize yourself with your local authority's copyright agreement.
Post relevant information near photocopiers and bring it to the attention of staff.

Confidentiality and disclosure

Pupil records and the courts

School staff are required to maintain confidentiality with respect to the contents of a record that comes to their knowledge in the course of their duties.

Parents of a pupil have access to the pupil's records if the pupil is younger than 18 years of age. Parent volunteers at the school and governing body members do not have access to information contained in pupil records other than those of their own children.

If you are asked to produce in court the records of a current or former pupil, seek legal advice through your school solicitor or from your local authority lawyer regarding disclosure and court procedures. Contact your professional association. If it is determined that you should provide records to the court, take the original and a photocopy with you, and request that the copy be submitted. If the production of school records is directed by a subpoena or summons, produce only those records expressly demanded by the court document and only if and when directed to do so by the judge.

Confidential information and the courts

Headteachers, teachers and other school professionals (for example, social workers) often have information communicated to them in confidence by pupils. Education-related and child protection legislation imposes specific duties of confidentiality on educators. In addition, various professional codes of ethics provide guidance regarding confidentiality matters for teachers, counsellors, social workers and psychologists, among others. Concomitant with the duty to maintain pupil confidentiality is the equally important, and at times supervening, duty of disclosure in certain circumstances as prescribed by case law. The issue of disclosure of information imparted in confidence is sensitive and complex.

If you are required to attend court for any reason, seek prior legal advice through your school's solicitor or from the local authority's lawyer, and contact your professional association for advice and assistance. If you believe you may be asked to disclose confidential information by the court, discuss this with your lawyer and your professional association in advance.

Confidentiality and the duty to report

The law in most applications makes it clear that educators have a duty to report to the local child protection officer if they have reason to suspect (or information regarding) a child who is or may be in need of protection. This applies even though the information may be confidential or privileged. Follow your local authority's procedures regarding reporting suspected child abuse and neglect. See Chapter 24, 'Protecting our Pupils', for further information.

Pupil records

It is the duty of the headteacher of a school to:

1. Establish, maintain, retain, transfer and dispose of a record for each pupil enrolled in the school in compliance with the policies established by the local authority.
2. Ensure that the materials in the pupil records are collected and stored in accordance with the policies established by the local authority.
3. Ensure the security of the pupil records.
4. Ensure that all staff responsible for performing clerical functions with respect to the establishment and maintenance of the pupil records are aware of the confidentiality provisions in Education Acts and the relevant freedom of information and data protection legislation.

Handling pupil records

Each time you handle a pupil record, for whatever reason, review its contents and organization. In this way you are conducting your own informal audit of the pupil records in the school. At the same time, you are learning more about the pupils and about the staff members who have prepared the documents in the pupil records.

TIP

Pupil records and record-keeping regarding violent incidents, bullying incidents or racial incidents

Follow your local authority's procedures as well as any relevant legislation regarding record-keeping and violent incidents.

Develop the documentation habit

Written records must be specific; note the date, time, place, and people involved. Take care to be accurate, factual, and objective.
The documentation is not completed until it is filed.
Note in the document where it is to be kept (filed) and who has copies.

TIP

Legislation regarding records and information management

Several pieces of legislation (and guidelines) have an impact on records and information management in the school. Consult your local authority policy and procedures and seek advice from your professional association to ensure you are familiar with and are following these policies and procedures.

Management of confidential information

Staff in schools often receive confidential information about pupils and adults in the community. This may include information disclosed to school representatives by police or court officers where the disclosure is necessary to ensure compliance of the young person with a court order, or to ensure the safety of staff, pupils or other persons. A pupil may inform staff they are pregnant; a pupil may disclose they are HIV positive; a headteacher may be told there is a sex offender living near the school. The school member of staff receiving such information should not disclose the information to any person other than the headteacher, who will decide what action is required to ensure the safety of staff, pupils, teachers or other persons. The headteacher should always seek advice from appropriate groups before taking any action related to the nature of the confidential information.

The Freedom of Information Act and the Data Protection Act

The Freedom of Information Act and the Data Protection Act exist to:

- provide a right of access to information produced by public authorities in the course of their business; this will include maintained schools
- protect the privacy of individuals with respect to personal information held by the employer and other organizations
- provide individuals with a right of access to that information.

Follow your local authority's procedures regarding freedom of information and data protection.

The Freedom of Information Act, in essence, allows an individual the right to access information provided by a public authority, including a school, in the conduct of their business. There are various exclusions whereby some information may be withheld, but generally it is assumed that most information is available to be disclosed. The Information Commissioner would, ultimately, reach a judgement on any request that was refused.

The Data Protection Act allows an individual to have a copy of any information held about them by an organization in a structured format. The individual will also be entitled to know how, when and where the information is stored, who can access it, for what purpose it is being retained and for how long, and can challenge any aspect of the management of the information.

Photographs

It is not unlawful to take a picture of someone or something. The use to which that picture or video footage is put might, however, be open to challenge. All subjects of pictures are lawfully entitled under Data Protection legislation to have a copy of the picture (information) held about them, and to know for what purpose the picture is taken. Hence the phone number adjacent to all closed-circuit television (CCTV) monitoring cameras, through which enquiries can be made.

Photographs of school pupils in brochures, on the web, at school plays, at sport events or swimming galas, by school staff, parents or the media in general can be used. If there is some evidence that such photos might lead to a significant risk to vulnerable adults or children, for example, those on witness protection schemes, then the school would be entitled to manage or even ban the photography or the distribution of any pictures.

Child protection and child abuse information

It is essential that you follow your local authority's procedures regarding reporting suspected child abuse and neglect. Failure to do so may bring harm to a child and could expose you to employment sanctions. Any concerns should be raised with the lead officer for child protection in the local authority by telephone or in writing. Keep a record of conversations with the lead officer, including the name of the officer, the date and time of the call, and the decision of whether the matter will be investigated, and by whom. In the course of making the report, you must disclose all necessary identifying information concerning the pupil so that the lead officer can fully investigate and take whatever steps they deem necessary in accordance with the Local Safeguarding Children Board (LSCB). The duty to report will almost always supersede any duty of confidentiality.

Duty to report a child in need of protection
If a person, including a person who performs professional or official duties with respect to children, has reasonable grounds to suspect abuse, the person must ensure that a report of the suspicion and the information on which it is based is made to the local child protection officer in the local authority.

In most cases this will be via the headteacher. However, if the headteacher is not the reporting person they must be copied into the referral.

MAKE DECISIONS WISELY

Do not be afraid to say, 'I don't know'.
Do not always feel that you have to have an answer on the spot. Especially in tight situations that are sensitive or political, buy yourself time. Say to the parent or individual, 'Let me look into that and gather the necessary information. I'll get back to you.'
Then get on and deal with it.

10 Budget and Resource Management

School budget: an overview

Among the many responsibilities associated with the role of the headteacher is the financial management of the school. This chapter will assist you in understanding your role in the financial procedures and point you in the right direction as you contemplate decisions regarding school budgets, spending and controls.

Local financial procedures spell out the financial responsibilities of the headteacher. The local authority will have certain policies and procedures in place to enforce and clarify the intent of the procedures.

Most authorities will have comprehensive documentation on all these issues in the form of financial management procedures, delegated budget management and audit requirements. It is especially important for newly appointed headteachers and deputy headteachers to become familiar with these documents.

This chapter attempts to highlight key elements of control, accountability and good practice.

Conflict of interest

A conflict of interest may arise where a person in authority is involved in an activity that can result in personal gain to himself or herself, to a family member or to a close associate. An example could involve the purchase of school materials from a relative, without involving the open competitive purchasing process. Another example would be a purchase for the school, made from a company that the person in authority owns or has an interest in. This can have serious consequences for the employee or the person in authority. Any employee or governor at risk of an accusation of conflict of interest, should declare the 'interest' and remove themselves from active involvement in the activity.

Local financial responsibility

The governing body has a delegated budget which is to be used for expenditure for the overall purpose of educating the pupils. The budget is set annually by the governing body to provide for the staffing, the running of the site, educational resources and the strategic development of the school. A move to multi-year budgets will help long-term planning. The headteacher implements the governors' budgetary policy.

TIP

> **Transparency and accountability**
> These are two key concepts to keep in mind when developing and managing your school budget.

School budgets

Each local authority receives from central government an allocation that is considered to be the appropriate amount for the authority to expend on its schools – the Dedicated Schools Grant (DSG). The authority can choose to add to this allocation, to reflect local priorities, but cannot take away from it. The DSG together with any additional monies becomes known as the Dedicated Schools Budget and it is this that is allocated to schools' budgets via the authority's funding formula. Some element of this can be held centrally – but only for direct expenditure on pupils, such as elements of the special needs statementing process.

Some local authorities allow schools to purchase or buy back services if they wish, with a service level agreement. Foundation, voluntary aided, trust and academy schools have more freedom to buy in services from any provider. Independent schools use fee revenue plus endowments to source services.

It is the aim of the governing body to stay within the school's budget. The headteacher may allocate amounts to each department or control it all in the headteacher's office, but the bottom line is that a headteacher should plan to stay within the total allocation. A deficit budget or a planned (or unplanned) overspend will attract Audit and Ofsted's attention and require a 'recovery' plan. The school should provide the governing body with monthly financial reports to help them monitor their spending. The Governing Body Finance Committee should review spending patterns, authorize virement between headings and check for financial probity in the management of the expenditure.

Your priority for decision-making when allocating funds and resources is the impact on pupil learning.

Consider:
- Is this decision in the best interest of the pupils?
- Is this decision aligned with our current priorities as expressed in the school development plan?

TIP

Petty cash fund

Petty cash provides a small sum of money to schools, which allows them to buy small items directly rather than through the school's purchasing scheme. Depending on the size of the school, funds may range from a few hundred pounds to a few thousand. The funds are charged against the school budget. Check your insurance policy to see the maximum cash that the school can hold in its safe.

A bank account requiring two signatures and held in the name of the school is recommended. If cash needs to be held in the school, it must be held securely. There is a requirement for monthly bank statements, supporting receipts and regular bank reconciliations to satisfy the school and the auditors that the funds are being controlled properly.

This petty cash fund must not be used to provide loans to staff and should be kept separate from any unofficial funds as described below. Consult your local authority finance team and/or auditors for guidance.

Owing to the cash issue, tight controls are a requirement and the petty cash fund is subject to audit. It is important to monitor and balance this fund on a regular basis.

As a supplement to petty cash, some schools use credit cards for small purchases. These purchase cards work like a personal Visa or Mastercard and are charged to the school budget. Controls over usage and safeguarding of the card(s) are the responsibility of the headteacher.

Expense reimbursement

Reimbursement for items such as mileage requires proper documentation and timely submission, at least on a quarterly basis, to ensure that it is charged to the correct budget year.

Funds that are not part of the delegated budget

Schools may also have access to funds that are raised or collected from sources other than the delegated budgets of the local authority. Depending on the school's geographic area (urban or rural), community involvement, and so on, the fund-raising activities may be modest or substantial. It is important to spell out the purpose, intended disposition and time frame for the fund-raising activity before it takes place to avoid any disagreements.

There are two general categories of these funds, and different groups are responsible for ensuring that they are used as intended. Local authority policy should further clarify the expectations and responsibilities of each group.

School non-delegated fund

School-administered funds are, for example, funds raised for pupil activities, field trips or special events. They are under the direct responsibility and authority of the headteacher. Certain basic controls are recommended, including:

- a bank account separate from petty cash
- a requirement for two signatures on the cheques
- bank reconciliations
- a proper filing of source documents.

The bookkeeping system can parallel that of petty cash. The school office/ finance officer looks after this account. Financial controls should be maintained, and, where funds are raised for a specific purpose, there is an obligation to ensure that they are expended for that purpose.

The overall budget and annual reviews should include delegated funds and non-delegated funds even if the expenditure patterns are combined.

Parent Teacher Association (PTA) funds

All fund-raising must adhere to local authority policy and regulation, and be used for the educational benefit of current pupils.

The headteacher must be able to advise, direct or even veto PTA funds which they wish to donate, but which would be for a purpose incompatible with the school development plan. For turnover of greater than £1000, the PTA should be registered with the Charity Commission and have in place a Trust Deed to regularize their financial business.

Audit

All financial activity of the school is subject to audit on a random, scheduled or targeted basis, either internally by school staff or externally by the district auditor. As a result, it is important to ensure that proper procedures and record-keeping are maintained.

Insurance

In most cases the local authority has property insurance coverage for the school building and liability insurance for potential issues related to staff, pupils and visitors. It is the headteacher's responsibility to inspect the building on a regular basis and to report deterioration or safety matters. Injury or threat of lawsuits should be communicated immediately to the appropriate local authority departments to ensure proper coverage and response. Lawsuits can implicate those indirectly responsible (headteacher, local authority) as well as those perceived to be directly responsible. For non-community schools the governing body/proprietor will need to arrange insurance, including legal cover. It is not usual to pay for insurance cover for pupils' personal belongings.

Asset management

The headteacher is responsible for the safekeeping of the assets of the school, including the following:

- furniture
- equipment
- computers
- books, and so on.

It is essential that schools maintain an inventory of these assets to assist in any insurance claims and to help the teaching staff monitor the equipment under their direct control. Assets that are deemed surplus to the school should be disposed of under the Local Authority Financial Management Regulations.

Transfer of school headteacher

It is important when a headteacher transfers from one school to another, or retires, that he or she leaves the school in good financial order for the new headteacher, including a reconciled bank account and a healthy budget position. This includes the transfer of signing authorities on any school bank account(s). The 'do unto others' adage applies; you would not want to inherit a school with financial problems.

Headteachers must follow local authority finance department direction faithfully and seek assistance whenever necessary. In non-community schools the local authority may well offer helpful advice.

Caution should be the watchword when it comes to financial management.

The governors' purchasing policy

The policy spells out the authority of the governing body, with respect to the competitive process, tendering and cost thresholds above which governing body decisions are needed rather than headteacher or school budget holder. It is especially important in a public organization funded by the taxpayer to ensure that there are equal opportunities for companies to bid and obtain contracts for the provision of goods and services, in addition to securing the best pricing.

Contracts

A contract with an individual or company is legally binding. Contracts therefore should be controlled and authorized centrally by the school in conjunction with the local authority. Considerations include the following:

- length of contract
- terms and penalties
- local authority standards.

It is important to note that a contract stays with the school; therefore, if a headteacher is transferred, the new headteacher is bound by the existing contract that may limit his or her options for the future.

Technology

Technology is exciting, and it can be difficult to resist the bargain at the local electronics store if you have sufficient funds in your budget. Stop! Technology is probably the one of the largest portions of the delegated school budget, after salaries and building maintenance. Adherence to area-wide standards of hardware, software and network is critical. The local authority contract may include items such as multi-year warranty, software loading, network standards and, possibly, training. Impulse purchases of information and communications technology (ICT) equipment can cause additional expense to the local authority as a whole and may not be supportable by your information technology advisers from county hall.

⊙ Tips regarding budget and resource management

1. Monitor your supply teacher budget closely. Inform your governing body if you have concerns that it will not last the year.

    (a) Follow policy to allocate and monitor the professional development funds for staff.
    (b) Monitor the photocopier budget closely; it can get away from you quickly.
    (c) Add an appropriate percentage to every purchase order to cover applicable taxes as well as shipping and handling costs; this eliminates nasty surprises when the invoice arrives.

2. Find out to what extent capital expenditure as well as building maintenance is a school budget item. Determine what you must fund; for example, you need to know who pays for the soap in the washrooms and the salt for the icy parking area. Find out how major repairs (for example, roof repairs) are funded. Consult the local authority's Asset Management Plan.

3. Apprise yourself of additional sources of local funds and how to access them. For example:

   (a) Standards funds and grants to be bid for, from local and national government
   (b) Centrally held special education funds
   (c) Funds accessible through bids submitted by individual schools
   (d) Professional development funds
   (e) Charitable organizations who can donate funds
   (f) Local business sponsorship
   (g) Fund-raising from ex-pupils/parents
   (h) Business opportunities to increase revenue – extended schools services, consultancies, and so on.

4. Follow local authority policy regarding unofficial funds. All fund-raising must adhere to local authority policy, whether it is school or PTA generated. Follow your local authority's procedures regarding accounting for unofficial funds; they will be audited.

   (a) Cash and cheques collected by the school from pupils and staff for:

      (i) materials supplied by pupils for lessons
      (ii) walk-a-thons and read-a-thons; sponsored events
      (iii) concerts and entertainment events
      (iv) sports fees
      (v) uniform sales
      (vi) collections from pupils and parents for field trips and off-site visits
      (vii) vending machine sales and proceeds from cafeteria operations
      (viii) school photo charges
      (ix) donations received from governing body activities.

   (b) School-generated funds raised through fundraising that is:

      (i) school administered (under the direct control of the headteacher)
      (ii) PTA administered (where the PTA has signing authority).

5. Find out if:

   (a) there are any other unofficial funds available in the school, which you may not know about

    (b) the school is involved in any partnerships or cooperative ventures

    (c) the school is the recipient of any sponsorships or donations.

6. Make effective use of volunteers, student teachers and work experience students; they support student and staff learning. You may use community resources to augment school resources. Exercise caution in this regard and be sure to follow local authority procedures.

7. Review local authority policy and ask the finance officer (and other appropriate staff) to brief you on past practice at the school regarding:

    (a) Local Authority Financial Management Regulations
    (b) school budgeting and accounting
    (c) requisitions and purchase orders
    (d) petty cash and purchase of low-value items
    (e) bank accounts and signing authority
    (f) the school safe and combination
    (g) the use of technology to support resource management and budget processes
    (h) school credit cards (purchasing cards).

Ensure that practices conform to local authority policy.

8. Familiarize yourself with the process for ordering, storing and distributing:

    (a) pupil consumables – for example, paper and art supplies
    (b) staff consumables – for example, staplers and computer disks.

Monitor inventories of consumables as well as furniture and equipment inventories; for example, computers, athletic equipment, musical instruments. Look at value for money; ask staff how consumable items can be justified in improving pupil learning and what alternatives have been considered.

9. Ask the site staff to brief you on all aspects of resource management concerning the physical plant. Encourage and support suggestions from all staff, pupils and parents to reduce inefficiencies and maximize cost-effectiveness; for example, ways to reduce paper use or fuel consumption.

10. Introduce yourself to finance staff at the local authority who are responsible for:

(a) school budget accounts
(b) purchasing
(c) online budget inquiry system
(d) school maintenance and repairs.

Do not hesitate to ask local authority staff for information, advice and assistance. When in doubt, contact your local authority office or help desk. And be mindful of educational value for money. Just because the school has always spent £x on educational provision, it does not meant that £x always has to be spent. Is there an alternative way of meeting the provision, maybe for less cost? If the learning objective is for pupils to understand 'life in the trenches' then a number of less or more expensive options exist:

(a) a visit to the Somme
(b) a video
(c) a textbook
(d) a visit from an 'old soldier'
(e) a museum
(f) a worksheet
(g) a website
(h) a role-play exercise.

All these resources will deliver some aspects of the learning experience, 'life in the trenches', but which is the most cost-effective and provides best value for money?

DELEGATE

Know when to ask for help. Don't believe that if you do it all yourself, then you must be a good administrator.
Hire some temporary office help for the really busy times, if you can.
Take time to find and train the right people; this pays off many times over in the future when you need assistance.
Delegate, but don't abdicate.

11 Technology

Getting started

Using technology effectively is an integral part of almost every aspect of the head-teacher's job. This chapter will provide a brief overview of several technology issues that you may wish to consider as a new headteacher or as a headteacher new to a school.

Getting orientated in your new school

1. Review
Review your local authority policies and procedures regarding computers, information technology, software, school websites, pupil and staff use of the

Internet, and other related issues. Review relevant school policies and procedures and the school's Information and Communication Technology Plan. Are they aligned with local authority policies?

2. Prepare

Become familiar with your own computer in your new office. Get *all* the passwords you need and keep records of them in a safe place. Change personal passwords as appropriate. If you are new to the e-mail system (for example, First Class Client, GroupWise, Lotus Notes, Outlook), arrange to learn how to use it immediately. (Review 'Tips for communicating by e-mail' in Chapter 5.) Learn how to use other features of your office computer; for example, scheduling meetings in your electronic calendar, setting the meeting notifier alarm.

3. Meet

Local authority allocated technology support: call and introduce yourself before you need to make that first urgent call for help. If you are new to the area, arrange to meet with an experienced headteacher to discuss technology issues in the local schools.

Office coordinator: discuss the use of computers and technology in the office. Who is responsible for administrative tasks (for example, attendance, budget)?

Computer or ICT teacher: discuss the use of technology at the school. Identify past successes, current priorities, emerging issues and future concerns. Ask for a tour with a guided overview of the use of technology in the school.

Familiarize yourself as quickly as possible with the technology in your school as it relates to:

- you
- the staff and pupils
- the parents and broader community.

 Technology inventory

Review the school's inventory of information and communication technology equipment. Conduct your own informal technology inventory as you do a building walk-through. Enquire about items that you would expect to see but cannot find. Add to the list below as you find other items. These devices range from low-tech telephones to high-tech state-of-the-art scientific equipment.

Communication

Audio conferencing, video conferencing and web conferencing capabilities
Mobile phones
Desktop computers
E-mail system
Fax machines
Internet connections
Laptops
Voicemail system
Walkie-talkies
The phone system
Alarm systems

Visual

Digital cameras
Overhead projectors
Whiteboards – interactive
Televisions
Video cameras
Video monitors for announcements, security
Videocassette recorders (VCRs) and DVD recorders
Video players

Organizational

Handheld personal computers and electronic organizers

> Technology can be used to assist with school administration, classroom lessons and group presentations.

➔ Further considerations for getting started

Here are some issues for further consideration:

1. The school technology plan.
2. Technology and the curriculum.
3. Technology and school administration.

4. Technology and staff development.
5. The acquisition of new ICT.
6. The acquisition of new educational and administrative software.
7. The location and use of technological devices.
8. The maintenance of equipment.
9. The establishment and maintenance of an inventory for hardware and software.
10. The safe use of the Internet by students; 'acceptable use' policies for all users.

> **Safe use of the Internet**
> For further information regarding the safe use of the Internet, see the website list later in this chapter.

Technology and school administration

Administrative software

Familiarize yourself with the administrative software used throughout the school for reports, timetabling, special education documentation, word processing, budgets, library cataloguing and purchasing. You do not need to be able personally to use every piece of administrative software, but it is helpful to know what software is used, who uses it and for what purpose. It is also important to determine who the backup person is for a particular task (for example, daily online reporting of staff absences) in the event that the usual staff member is not available to undertake the task.

Personal productivity technology

Make a conscious effort to keep yourself up to date on new software and technology that you can use to make your own job easier. Software designed for word processing, accounting, timetabling, personal scheduling and data management is readily available and constantly updated. Find out what your experienced colleagues recommend, establish your priorities, and identify the new software programs and technologies that you want to master this year.

Using the Internet to assist you with your job

Use the Internet to conduct online research and to find specific information that you need to help you carry out your responsibilities. Bookmark your favourite sites and monitor them regularly.

1. Bookmark your local authority website for quick access to policies and procedures.
2. See the list of websites in the resources section at the end of this handbook for additional addresses.

> Check your local authority policy and procedures regarding acceptable use of computers and Internet or intranet technology and computer network security.

Technology and the curriculum

Specific uses of technology are usually incorporated into the National Curriculum at all levels. As a headteacher, you monitor the integration of technology into the curriculum when you observe the teaching and learning process, oversee pupil achievement, assess school curricula and evaluate staff performance. Becoming familiar with educational software used in the school is helpful. When you demonstrate an informed interest in information and communication technology, you encourage its use as a tool to support pupil and staff learning.

The role of technology in the curriculum: an overview

- *Information literacy* is the ability to access, select, gather, critically evaluate, create and communicate information, and to use the information obtained to solve problems and make decisions. In preparation for further education, employment, citizenship and lifelong learning, pupils must be capable of deriving meaning from information by using a wide variety of information literacy skills.
- As part of their training in computer and information literacy, pupils should become familiar with a range of available software programs, simulations, multimedia resources, databases and computer-assisted learning modules.
- Pupils will also be expected to use software applications that help them develop general skills in such areas as writing, problem-solving, research and communication.
- It is important that pupils learn to evaluate critically the accuracy, validity, currency, comprehensiveness and depth of the information they access using information technology, particularly the Internet.

- In general, teachers must try to ensure that pupils acquire the knowledge, skills and attitudes that will allow them to use computer and information technology safely, effectively, confidently and ethically.
- As the technology capable of enhancing pupil learning becomes available, teachers should, within a reasonable period of time, incorporate that technology into their planning of instruction and learning activities in individual disciplines and, collaboratively, across subject areas.
- Effective school library provision can also help to promote the development of information literacy skills among all pupils by supporting and coordinating the collaborative planning and implementation of reading programmes, inquiry and research tasks, and independent study.

Building your school technology plan

Once you have familiarized yourself with the current status of information technology in your new school, you will want to begin the process of planning for the future. Remember that a planning process was in place before you arrived, so you will be building on what went before. As in all areas of school improvement planning, you will want to acknowledge the work done to date.

Check your local authority policies and procedures regarding school technology plans. If your local authority has a template for school plans, follow it. Beyond that, think outside the box when developing your plan.

 Ten essential elements for developing an effective technology plan

1. Create a vision.
2. Involve all stakeholders.
3. Gather data.
4. Review the research.
5. Integrate technology into the curriculum.
6. Commit to professional development.
7. Ensure a sound infrastructure.
8. Allocate appropriate funding and budget.
9. Plan for ongoing monitoring and assessment.
10. Prepare for tomorrow.

Source: adapted from Barnett, 2001.

Remember to delegate when appropriate. You cannot do everything yourself, nor should you.

TIP

'If you have a technology planning committee, thank them for their contributions to date.

Re-engineer the process to plan for information and communication instead of technology.

Let go of the techno-centric focus:

What is out?	Technology Committee
What is in?	Information Communications Committee'

(November, 2001)

COMMUNICATE CONSTANTLY

Don't be afraid to over-communicate.

Ask yourself:

Who needs to know this?
How will I communicate it to them?
When do I need to communicate it?

12 The Governing Body

➔ Preparing to work with your governing body

The purpose of the governing body is to improve pupil achievement and to enhance the accountability of the education system to parents, and the local community.

- An effective school governing body can be one of your school's greatest assets. Establishing a positive working relationship with the governors is critical to the success of the school.

- The role of the governing body is to establish a strategic framework for the school by setting aims and objectives, and then setting policies and targets for achieving these aims and objectives.
- The governing body will monitor and evaluate progress towards achievement of the aims and objectives, and will regularly review the strategic framework in the light of that progress.
- They will consider any advice given by the headteacher, will support the headteacher in the performance of his/her functions and will give him/her constructive criticism.
- The headteacher will advise the governing body in relation to the establishment and review of the strategic framework, and will formulate aims, objectives, policies and targets for the governing body to adopt, modify or reject.
- The headteacher will be responsible for the internal organization, management and control of the school, and the implementation of the strategic framework.
- The headteacher will comply with any reasonable direction of the governing body in performing any function delegated to him/her by the governing body.

The above regulations are contained in the Education (School Government – Terms of Reference, England) Regulations 2000 and provide the legislative basis for the respective roles of the governing body and the headteacher.

Here are some steps to consider, whether you are new to the school or starting a school year with a new governing body in the same school. Begin by scanning the environment; don't start by jumping in and changing things.

Review current legislation and relevant documentation

Review any local authority policies and procedures regarding governing bodies; for example:

- the adoption of local authority personnel procedures for use by the governing body as employer
- community use of schools
- extended schools and federations, consortia, collaborations
- school transport
- child protection
- financial and budget management
- trips and visits
- health and safety
- expenses for governors
- admission and exclusion policies

- the local authority role in monitoring and intervening in schools causing concern
- clerking the governing body
- local authority governor services and their support for 'good practice'.

Also review the governing body's:

- terms of reference and remit; the clerk to the governors should be able to provide copies of the instruments and articles of government and the terms of reference for each committee
- annual report/school profile and minutes from the previous year
- newsletters from last year and articles in school newsletters.

Gather further information

If you are new to the school, invite key people to update you on governing body issues:

- deputy headteacher (*Note*: the deputy head often attends all governing body meetings.)
- chair of governors
- community governors
- bursar/business manager/school secretary
- clerk to the governors
- staff governor.

Working with your governing body

Getting underway

Meet with the chair to discuss goals, communication and other items.

1. *Goals*

    (a) Chair:
       (i) personal views and beliefs
       (ii) list of issues and concerns regarding the school and the governors.

(b) Headteacher:

  (i) personal views and beliefs and general goals
  (ii) list of issues and concerns regarding the school and the governors.

(c) Linking governing body activities and goals to pupil achievement.

2. *Communication*

  (a) Between headteacher and chair and governing body:

    (i) regular meetings
    (ii) telephone calls
    (iii) e-mails.

  (b) Between headteacher and community:

    (i) website
    (ii) newsletters
    (iii) local newspaper.

  (c) Between governing body and school staff:

    (i) governor newsletters
    (ii) bulletin board
    (iii) website.

3. *Administrative items*

(Check the appropriate local authority policies for these.)

- Composition of governing body: different categories of members including associate members.
- Consultation with parents of the school community.
- Understanding and agreement on dealing with disputes and protocols.
- Election of parent members and other members.
- Fund-raising.
- Meetings of the governing body: frequency, place, time, reports, preparation.
- Arrangements for committees: finance, staffing, curriculum, and so on.
- Term of office, vacancies and officers.
- Committee procedures, clerking, voting, minutes, resolutions.

Considering other issues

Be sure to take these issues into consideration when working with your governing body:

1. *Membership*

    (a) Recruiting, training, and retaining members of the governing body.
    (b) Achieving meaningful diversity on the governing body.

2. *Meetings*

    (a) Arranging logistics of group meetings (room, coffee, arrangement of furniture).
    (b) Running effective meetings.
    (c) Scheduling regular meetings with the chair (for example, once a week).
    (d) Working with the chair to prepare the agenda a week in advance of meetings.

3. *Process*

    (a) Developing strategies for setting goals and building consensus in the governing body.
    (b) Considering the role of individual governors in supporting and championing specific school developments.
    (c) Giving personal invitations for school events to the chair and the other governing body members.
    (d) Planning staff presentations to the governing body regarding curriculum, finance, strategies, and so on.

Finding a focus, clarifying goals

Clear goals bring people together and give them a purpose for collaborating. Your governing body may have too many priorities, unclear priorities or no priorities. The result may be little momentum, wasted resources and diminished support.

Possible goals for the school and/or the governing body include:

- To improve literacy.
- To improve pupil behaviour.
- To promote parental involvement.
- To improve the physical appearance of the school.
- To focus on healthy lifestyles.

Leading the governing body through the strategic focus can be very rewarding.

'The major focus of governing bodies is to support and enhance learning for all pupils by developing powerful partnerships between schools, families and communities.'

(M. Fullan, Dean, Ontario Institute for Studies in Education/University of Toronto)

The respective roles of the headteacher and the governing body

The headteacher is the lead professional in the school and is automatically an ex officio member of the governing body. The headteacher has a legal right to attend all committee meetings of the governing body and can only be required to leave a meeting if there is a clear conflict of interest between the headteacher's individual role as an employee and his/her role as governor. This would be rare but, for instance, would occur when the headteacher is facing a serious disciplinary matter and the relevant governor committee retires to consider its verdict.

The headteacher's ultimate role is to advise the governing body of the educational implications of any decisions they make. The governing body's role is to work at a strategic level and not to be involved in detailed school management, operational or confidential 'case' matters.

Occasionally a governors' appeal panel will sit and give a second, final opinion on a management matter, if procedures so allow. It is vital that governors do not involve themselves individually or collectively in management procedures at an earlier level, to avoid accusations of bias or tainting.

The triumvirate of the headteacher, chair and clerk is the powerhouse of the governor–school relationship. It is essential that these three work harmoniously together.

The clerk to the governors is a vital and senior role, and is the expert adviser to the governing body about all matters to do with procedure, remit, governance, protocols and the efficient conduct of business. The clerk should provide the organizational and secretariat service to the governing body, not the headteacher!

Individual governors have no power or authority to require or direct the headteacher to do anything. Even the chair has only limited power, in a few emergency situations, to take any action or executive decisions. If a committee wishes a particular course of action, it is helpful if a resolution is proposed and seconded and voted upon. Then it is legitimized.

Selection of the headteacher

One of the key and exclusive roles of the governing body is to select a new headteacher. The local authority can advise but the governing body has the ultimate responsibilities and power to select its chosen candidate.

Effective governing bodies

 Characteristics of effective governing bodies

Effective governing bodies:

- focus on pupil learning and the best interests of all pupils
- are actively involved in setting school priorities for improving pupil achievement
- promote meaningful parental and community involvement and actively seek the views of their school communities
- have a clear understanding of their roles and responsibilities
- include members who represent the diverse views of their school communities
- keep well informed about school and local authority policies and procedures
- have clear and consistent processes for decision-making
- communicate with the community about their activities
- maintain high ethical standards
- have members who have developed mutual trust and respect for one another.

> In many areas, particularly in urban centres where there is a greater ethnic mix, it is especially important to find ways of encouraging participation from the various and diverse ethno-cultural groups that make up the community.

What if disputes arise between members of the governing body?

School governing bodies may establish a protocol that, in accordance with any applicable policies established by the local authority, outlines a conflict resolution process for internal disputes. A conflict resolution process may have the headteacher perform the role of mediator or arbitrator, or it may rely on other local authority personnel to provide an outside perspective and relative impartiality in this regard. For further information, see Chapter 7, 'Managing Conflict and Difficult People'.

Governing bodies and confidentiality

Governing bodies are not entitled to receive confidential pupil information, nor is it appropriate for them to attempt to consult with headteachers or local authority personnel about decisions relating to individual pupils.

Headteachers should ensure that discussions about staffing remain general, without any focus on individual teachers. Remember that the agenda, minutes and papers relating to each committee meeting will eventually become available to members of the public, unless the committee determine with good reason that some minutes/papers remain confidential to members of the governing body actually present.

Attendance of non-governors at governing body meetings is entirely at the discretion of the governing body itself.

GET TO KNOW THE COMMUNITY

You may be invited to governing body meetings or school meetings before your new position commences. Certainly attend if you wish, but be careful about being drawn into any early position before you have a chance to verify the actuality when you are in post. The current headteacher is, after all, still in charge. Things are never quite what they seem.

13 School Organization and Timetabling

Getting started on the curriculum plan

Key questions

Before making any changes, ensure that you have gathered all relevant data. Any changes you make may be received with hostility, so proceed with caution. When it is time for you and your senior team to start working on next year's school organization and timetable, consider the following key questions.

1. What are the contractual obligations set out in the staff contracts?
2. What is your staffing allocation?
3. What flexibility do you have in the utilization of your staffing allocation?
4. How should the governors staffing committee, the unions, the whole staff and the governing body as a whole be involved in school organization and timetabling?
5. What are the goals for the school's curriculum plan?

6. What information and tools do you need to develop the plan and timetabling?
7. What are the steps in creating the curriculum plan?
8. What are the challenges in implementing the plan?
9. What models and approaches are currently being used?
10. How do class size and the school size affect timetabling?

Goals

Your goals for school organization and timetabling may include some of the following:

- increasing time in lessons for pupils and reducing transition time between lessons
- providing common planning time for teachers, and improved staff development opportunities
- offering programmes by specialist teachers (for example, physical and health education, music, sports, languages)
- implementing online courses and distance learning.

 A checklist

When you start planning your school curriculum plan and timetable, consider the following factors:

1. The National Curriculum requirements for your Key Stages. Looking at recommended time allowances or envelopes for an academic year.

   Exploring alternative models of delivery in terms of year-long weekly provision versus intensive front-loaded, or end-loaded concentrated time allocations in unequal time frames. Consider alternative models of year, class, group and individual arrangements for pupil tuition. Examine structures based on year groups and consider alternative groupings for certain learning activities: by gender, by ability, by preferred learning style. Think about extension opportunities for talented and gifted pupils, and extra support for those with challenging learning needs. Build in thinking about formative and summative assessments at critical times.

2. Having built a curriculum-led staffing model, examine the best fit of current staff to the model, looking at staff strengths rather than individual preferences. Remember, most staff can adapt to alternative year groups/teaching structures if they have to ... with appropriate in-service training (INSET). The contract is non-negotiable but the job description is, as school needs and situations change.

3. Forecast admissions profiles and pupil turbulence to get a picture of likely group sizes through the year(s). Build in relevant factors to do with exclusion, travellers' children, fluidity of the local population, looked-after pupils, and so on.

4. Revisit the management structure at intervals, examining how the support staff are enabled to provide all non-teaching support activities (for example, the '25' tasks) and examining how the teaching and learning responsibility (TLR) posts are contributing to more effective learning.

5. Ensure planning, preparation and assessment (PPA) time is in place, manageable, *not* at cost to the headteacher's own time, and evaluated.

6. Consider INSET requirements for the coming year's key strategic developments in the curriculum plan.

7. Evaluate the system and the software for organization planning, pupil progress monitoring, and timetabling.

8. Consider the increasing significance of the extended school agenda whereby some educational provision may be on alternative sites (hence causing transport issues), and the collaboration/federation issue whereby schools may 'cluster' together to provide common education.

9. How are specialist teachers/instructors able to visit and contribute to the maximum effectiveness?

10. Does the curriculum model lend itself to a thorough programme of lesson observations by senior staff and by peers?

11. Consider best use of technology and good practice to allow varied learning:

   (a) role play – acting out
   (b) use of video to analyze, embed learning
   (c) virtual reality/simulation software and ICT
   (d) lectures, seminars, pupil presentations and other formats
   (e) educational use of phone, fax, text, MSN, Internet, e-mail, and so on.

Management issues

Consult with staff. This means:

- acquaint them with the proposals and seek their comments/responses
- carefully consider their responses
- make a reasoned management decision having considered all advice

- promulgate and promote the 'plan'
- expect senior management team endorsement and encourage staff-wide ownership
- for any contentious proposals, consider a pilot scheme or one-term trial with a genuine review thereafter.

Consult with governing body:

- to check that proposals fall within the strategic framework
- the governors may pronounce on 'what' is to be achieved but the head-teacher and staff are responsible for 'how.'

Update:

- parents
- local authority
- the community at large
- sponsors, commercial partners, and so on
- and, not forgetting, the pupils who are going to be the eager recipients of the curriculum plan.

Implementation challenges

Constant change

Regardless of the degree of planning and monitoring, be prepared to deal with a number of challenges and unexpected events when managing the curriculum plan and timetabling. Develop strategies to address:

- parent requests for specific teachers or change of teachers or courses
- cancelled courses and programmes
- unanticipated increases or decreases in enrolment in September
- a key member of staff leaving at an inconvenient time or with short notice
- new school additions or renovations that might not be completed for September
- late budget changes
- the latest government initiative(s).

Class size and school size considerations

While the local authority gives information on the average class sizes for primary, special and secondary schools, you will want to be aware of the research on class size and school size. Review the research on class size, school size, multi-age groupings, and so on, if this is a priority. Understand the difference between average class size and the overall pupil–teacher ratio in the school when creating the school's curriculum plan. Class size does not refer to pupil–teacher ratio.

- Educate the staff, parents and governing body group about the effects of school size and class size on school effectiveness.
- Monitor class size to ensure it complies with legal requirements.
- If you have concerns, monitor and document the impact of school size on pupil achievement, support for pupils with special needs, school climate, staff productivity and burnout, pupil behaviour and discipline, and so on, and share these concerns with your school improvement partner (SIP).

Implementing a new school curriculum plan or timetabling model

1. Involve your local authority (LA) early in the process; changing the timetable might require LA approval, building renovations, transportation changes or staffing modifications.
2. Ensure sufficient time is allocated to gather information, consult all stakeholders, design and, if possible, field-test the model.
3. Consider creating a research or steering committee of staff, pupils and parents.
4. Survey staff, pupils and parents about their perspectives on the school's timetable and how it affects their family and work responsibilities, as well as pupil achievement.
5. Make certain that staff members understand the changes in educational strategies required with a particular organizational model.
6. Ensure staff have access to development activities that support implementation.
7. Keep the school governing body, staff, parents, pupils and teachers' unions informed in order to promote understanding and reduce conflict.

8. Keep in mind: required National Curriculum programmes of study (courses), course sequencing, number of instructional minutes in the day and the minutes per course or subject. In secondary schools, most pupils must be able to reach the national targets for Key Stage 3 and Key Stage 4 at the correct chronological age.

9. Design a procedure that will accommodate pupils transferring from a school with a different timetable or organizational structure.

10. Monitor the impact of any curriculum changes and share evaluation of the data with all stakeholders.

MANAGE CHANGE CAREFULLY

Don't change the school's organization or procedures right away. There are likely to be very good reasons for the way things are done. Go slowly with change. Everything does not have to be done immediately.

14 Inspection and Quality Assurance

At a glance

- Quality assurance models

  Features of quality assurance models
  Selecting the right quality scheme for your school
  Some examples of quality assurance frameworks

- School self-evaluation

  Features of effective school self-evaluation
  The self-evaluation form (SEF)
  Developing the school improvement plan

- Ofsted inspection

  What is the new Ofsted framework?
  What is being inspected?

Quality assurance models

The aim of quality assurance and quality improvement schemes is to maintain, or in some cases raise, standards by encouraging assessment of the service, comparing it with descriptions of best practice, and then identifying areas for improvement.

Features of quality assurance models

Quality assurance models usually include some form of assessment, which can be self-assessment and/or assessment by an independent assessor who judges whether the collected evidence meets specific accreditation criteria.

Those judged to have met the criteria are generally awarded the 'kitemark' or equivalent by the accrediting organization.

Some schools find it useful to work to a quality assurance (QA) scheme as it can:

- provide a clear framework for continuous improvement
- identify a goal for all to work to
- identify where gaps or problems exist
- bring teams together
- develop a completed portfolio or report that acts as an invaluable reference document for people and can be used in training new staff
- prepare you for local authority and Ofsted inspections.

Selecting the right quality scheme for your school

The following questions may help you decide which QA model would best support your school improvement process:

- Do you need an external accreditation to work to?
- Does the model fit the context you are in and is it 'fit for purpose'?
- What are the associated benefits and costs and will the outcomes be worth the effort?
- What will be the expected impact on pupils' learning and teaching?
- What model is more accepted or well respected within education?
- Does your local authority, or any contract/funding you are working to, require a particular approach to QA?
- What will be the advantages/disadvantages of working to the QA model?

Some examples of quality assurance frameworks

The Investors in People (IiP) standard
The Investors in People (IiP) standard is a business improvement tool designed to advance an organization's performance through its people. It has been both applied and adapted for use in schools, and many schools have been evaluated and hallmarked with the IiP award. The website www.investorsinpeople.co.uk provides further information about the standard.

Charter Mark
The Charter Mark is the government's national standard for excellence in customer service. Organizations that undertake the formal assessment

process are independently evaluated and assessed against six criteria focusing on customers and aiming to constantly improve. More information about the Charter Mark can be found at www.cabinetoffice.gov.uk/chartermark.

National Healthy Schools Standard (NHSS)

The aim of the NHSS is to improve educational achievement, health and emotional well-being, and make schools safe, secure and healthy environments, in which pupils can learn and develop. The standards cover eight key areas of activity and can be achieved at three levels. Further details about the NHSS can be found from your local authority adviser or at www.standards.gov.uk.

The Quality Mark

The Basic Skills Quality Mark provides a framework for schools to improve what they are doing in terms of basic skills: reading, writing, spelling and maths. Working in partnership, the Basic Skills Agency supports the local authority to assess their schools against the ten elements of the award. Further information about the Basic Skills Quality Mark can be found at www.basic-skills.co.uk.

School self-evaluation

Effective schools have always worked hard to ensure that regular self-review, linked to school planning, has learning and teaching at the heart of the process.

School review/self-evaluation has become all the more important as it is now a key feature of the 'New Relationship with Schools' (NRwS) agenda for all schools to improve their own performance through 'intelligent accountability' based upon a more effective use of self-evaluation.

The challenge for school leaders is to ensure that both the school self-evaluation process and the report supports continuous improvement and is embedded in the culture of the school.

Features of effective school self-evaluation

1. Does the self-evaluation identify how well our school serves its learners?
2. How does our school compare with the best schools, and the best comparable schools?
3. Is the self-evaluation integral to our key management systems?
4. Is our school self-evaluation based on a good range of telling evidence?

---

5. Does our school's self-evaluation and planning involve key people in the school and seek the views of parents, learners and external advisors and agencies?
6. Does our school's self-evaluation lead to action to support the school's longer term goals for development?

(*A New Relationship with Schools – Improving Performance Through School Self-evaluation*, DfES/Ofsted, June 2006)

The self-evaluation form (SEF)

TIP

When writing a self-evaluation report, remember that it needs to convey a clear picture of how well the school is doing, provide clear proof of how you know what you know, show what you are doing to build on success and remedy weaknesses.

When completing the SEF remember:

- *Think* – what are the key messages you want to convey? How would you summarize the finding to a new governor or an interested parent? What about the outcomes for pupils? Has the school met the five outcomes of the *Every Child Matters* (ECM) agenda?
- *Browse* – the interactive SEF website, www.ofsted.gov.uk/schools/sef. cfm#schools, has lots of useful information.
- *Read* – guidance on the Ofsted website and work your way through the tutorial.
- *Evaluate* – remember to analyse the impact of what you do.

Before you submit a SEF:

1. Read it through.
2. Is it short and to the point?
3. Have you answered all the questions?
4. Are your judgements clear?
5. Have you reflected stakeholders' views?
6. Does it give a fair and honest picture of what the school is like?
7. Have you been clear about the actions being taken to improve?
8. If you were an inspector what questions would your SEF lead you to ask?
   Source: adapted from *Writing a SEF that Works*, Ofsted, 2006.

Developing the school improvement plan

Key features of effective plans

- Based on evidence
- Focused on no more than 3–5 goals
- Practical and achievable
- Measured and timed
- Monitored and evaluated
- High impact strategies
- Collaboration
- Unrelenting focus on teaching and learning
                        (*Handbook for School Improvement Partners*, Ofsted, 2004)

Ofsted inspection

Undergoing an Ofsted inspection can be a daunting prospect for any head-teacher and his/her school. However, it can be made less daunting by ensuring that your school self-evaluation processes are effective, and by being prepared for the inspection.

What is the new Ofsted framework?

The 2005 Inspection Framework provides a radically different system for school inspections. The main differences are:

- short inspections of no more than two days and smaller inspection teams
- short notice (normally two days) of inspection to avoid unnecessary preparation
- three years as the usual period between inspections
- strong emphasis on self-evaluation as the starting point for inspection
- required input from pupils, parents and other stakeholders
- a common inspection framework for all schools and post-16 colleges.

What is being inspected?

Inspectors must report on:

- the quality of the education provided in the school
- how far the education meets the needs of the range of pupils at the school
- the educational standards achieved in the school
- the quality of the leadership in, and management of the school, including whether the financial resources made available to the school are managed efficiently
- the extent to which schools are developing rigorous internal procedures of self-evaluation
- the spiritual, moral, social and cultural development of the pupils at the school
- the contribution made by the school to the well-being of those pupils
- the behaviour and attendance of pupils.

Pre-inspection

- Get the self-evaluation process and the SEF right – involve all the staff in self-evaluation of departments and the whole school
- Keep the SEF updated
- Practise paired observations of lessons
- Survey pupils', governors' and parents' opinions as part of a regular planning cycle – don't wait for Ofsted
- When you get the phone call, don't panic – stay positive
- Focus on the pupils – it's all about them after all

('An inspector calls', www.teachernet.gov.uk, 2005)

Further information on Ofsted inspections is available at www. ofsted. gov.uk.

PART 2
Teaching and Learning

15 School curriculum

Getting started

Building a learning community

What is a learning community?
Building a learning community in your school focuses on creating an environment where all see themselves as learners. 'An effective professional learning community has the capacity to promote and sustain the learning of professionals in the school community with the collective purpose of

enhancing pupil learning' (DfES RR 637, 2005, p. 3). It is about individuals who share a common vision of the learning environment they want to create. It is about individuals who form dynamic learning collaboratives, which explore, discover and share in the design of a road map for their journey of learning. Creative ideas and solutions are stimulated and fostered. Collective thinking and action is required. Progress is expected and measured. Challenges and obstacles provide more opportunities to learn. It is all about passion, commitment and the belief that you can create your own vision for learning in an effective school.

A professional learning community is built rigorously upon the foundations of:

- *Mission* – Why do we exist?
- *Vision* – What do we hope to become?
- *Values* – How must we behave?
- *Goals* – What steps and when?

Building a professional learning community requires schools to examine and respond to the key questions surrounding the four foundations. As curriculum leaders, headteachers must begin their journey with an understanding and commitment to this process. Patience and persistence will keep them on course.

How to build one in your school

Step one is to form learning teams or alliances. These are small groups of professionals who agree to experiment with new ideas and meet regularly for a specific period of time to share experiences guided by specific goals and purposes. The requirements for effective learning teams are collaboration, effective inquiry, action orientation and experimentation. The effort to transform a school into a professional learning community is more likely to be sustained when teachers:

- participate in reflective dialogue
- observe and respond to one another's teaching
- jointly develop curriculum and assessment practices
- work together to implement new programmes and strategies
- share lesson plans and material
- collectively engage in problem-solving, action research and continuous improvement practices.

The headteacher's role is to facilitate the work of learning by creating time and the ethos and environment that empower teachers to collaborate. This can be done by examining the school schedule and finding ways to free up time for meetings. The headteacher needs actively to show interest and ensure that anyone, regardless of experience or age, can participate.

On a cyclical basis, the learning community, led by the headteacher, must review and assess achievement of goals, reflect on results, refocus on mission, vision and values, and revise the school improvement plan accordingly.

Reviewing school programmes

1. Review your local authority's policies and procedures related to school programmes, curriculum and pupil achievement.
2. Review curriculum programmes.

   (a) What curriculum provision is offered at your school?
   (b) How many pupils are enrolled in each programme?
   (c) Invite key staff members to brief you on each of the instructional programmes.

3. Find out about the following:

   (a) the curriculum currently offered at the school
   (b) the history of activities at the school.

4. Obtain copies of all relevant curriculum documents.
5. Review the course outlines and long-range plans for all courses offered at the school.
6. As you read pupils' reports and review them with teachers, you will learn a lot about school curriculum, individual pupil success, overall levels of pupil achievement, and the quality of pupil assessment, evaluation and reporting at the school.
7. Be visible in the school; observe teaching and learning in action.

Pulling it all together

As a school leader, you will pull together your knowledge and skills from a number of key areas in order to support school programmes and pupil learning. These include your knowledge and skills in the following key areas:

Programme

- Current research.
- National and local policies and procedures.
- Curriculum and expectations.
- Scheduling and school organizational structures.
- Creative use of school facilities.

Teachers

- Teaching and learning styles; brain-friendly teaching and learning.
- Staffing (selection and assignment).
- Teacher performance management.
- Staff development.

Students

- Characteristics of pupils at different stages of development.

Policy

- Inclusion, cultural equity, and antidiscrimination and antiviolence education.
- Pupil assessment, evaluation, and reporting practices and procedures.
- Assessment, evaluation and the utilization of data.
- Budgeting that supports learning priorities.
- School profile and goals based on standardized testing results.

Curriculum implementation

The headteacher's role (refer to the National Standards for Headteachers)

As the headteacher, you will lead the curriculum implementation process at the school.

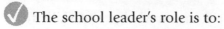 The school leader's role is to:

- set the vision and mission (in consultation with all stakeholders)
- provide staff development
- motivate, coach and set expectations

- provide resources and time
- identify ways to motivate curriculum discussion
- model desired behaviours and attitudes.

➔ Curriculum implementation timelines

In concert with local authority directions, support a curriculum implementation timeline over a three- to five-year cycle. Remember, implementation is a process, not an event. Share this timeline with all stakeholders.
  Determine timelines for each stage of implementation:

- familiarization
- initial introduction
- partial implementation
- continuing implementation
- full implementation.

Determine timelines for each stage of curriculum review:

- initial reactions
- ongoing, formative review
- final, summative review.

Assessment and evaluation of programmes: data-driven improvement

Teachers and headteacher's should systematically review:

- course content
- teaching/learning strategies and
- assessment procedures,

and make the changes needed to improve their students' achievements.
  The analysis of the results of:

- local assessments
- local authority wide assessments and
- national and international testing

provides additional information on pupil achievement and programme effectiveness, complementing the programme assessments conducted by teachers and headteacher.

Where areas for improvement are identified through such analysis, schools and local authorities should work with parents and other representatives from the community to address these areas in their school and local authority action plans.

Assessing the implementation of the curriculum

The local authority may recommend a process for assessing curriculum implementation. You and your staff may wish to design rubrics using performance levels and expectations.

Just beginning	Approaching implementation	Fully implementing	Extensively implementing
I use some …	*I use many …*	*I regularly use …*	*I effectively use and develop …*

Expectations you may wish to assess include, among others:

- planning, organizing and delivering programmes based on overall and specific expectations
- designing performance tasks to assess multiple expectations across the achievement categories
- planning programme activities that include expectations from various subjects
- using a range of teaching/learning strategies and appropriate resources to deliver programmes
- ensuring that the individual learning needs of all pupils are met.

Pupil assessment, evaluation and reporting

As you monitor the implementation of the curriculum, you will also want to monitor pupil assessment and evaluation practices and the reporting of pupil achievement.

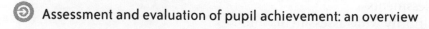 Assessment and evaluation of pupil achievement: an overview

The primary purpose of assessment and evaluation is to improve pupil learning. Assessment and evaluation are based on the curriculum expectations and the achievement levels outlined in the curriculum policy document for each subject.

In order to ensure that assessment and evaluation are valid and reliable, and that they lead to the improvement of pupil learning, teachers must use appropriate strategies. The items below can be used as a checklist to help you monitor the assessment and evaluation strategies being used in your school.

Teachers must use strategies that:

- address both wha] learn and how well they learn
- are based both on the development of knowledge and skills and on agreed achievement level descriptions
- are varied in nature, administered over a period of time and designed to provide opportunities for pupils to demonstrate the full range of their learning and achievement
- are appropriate for the learning activities used, the purposes of teaching/ learning and the needs and experiences of the students
- are fair to all students
- accommodate the needs of capable students, consistent with the strategies outlined in any individual education plans
- accommodate the needs of pupils for whom the medium of teaching and learning is not their first language
- ensure that each pupil is given clear directions and targets for improvement
- promote pupils' ability to assess their own learning and to set specific goals
- include the use of samples of pupils' work that provide evidence of their achievement
- are communicated clearly to pupils and parents at the beginning of the course and at other appropriate points throughout the course.

Reporting pupil achievement

Reports
Follow your local authority's guidelines regarding reporting pupil achievement. Pupil achievement must be communicated formally to pupils and parents by means of a reporting system. Provide staff with guidelines and timelines for the completion of any reports. Provide training regarding the completion of electronic reports for staff who are new to the technology.

Provide regular training for all staff to develop consistency in pupil assessment, evaluation and reporting. This will involve moderation discussions regarding specific curriculum expectations, levels of achievement, assessment rubrics, pupil work samples, and so on. Facilitate communication among the various teachers who report on a pupil's achievement.

Read and sign pupil reports. Share this task with the deputy head as appropriate. Follow up where necessary.

Meet with teachers individually to discuss the quality of their reporting and the achievement of individual students.

Parent–teacher meetings

Encourage and support teachers as they conduct parent–teacher meetings. Provide staff with training for conducting successful parent conferences. Find or create a list of suggestions and share them at a staff meeting. Both new teachers and experienced teachers will benefit from these discussions.

Parents' meeting tips should include what to do before, during and after a parent interview to ensure its success. Timekeeping is often an issue.

Ongoing reporting to parents

In addition to reports and scheduled school-wide parent–teacher meetings, encourage teachers to communicate with parents when necessary through a variety of strategies, and support them in this process. Strategies, depending on the school and parent practice might include informal notes, daily feedback in some circumstances, communication books and pupil agendas, phone calls, class newsletters and e-mails. The goal is to keep parents informed and to avoid surprises.

English as a second language and English for speakers of other languages: getting started

Review the local authority's:

- policies and procedures regarding English as a Second Language (ESL) and English for Speakers of Other Languages (ESOL)
- handbook
- forms
- parent brochures
- process for assessment and placement of incoming ESL/ESOL pupils.

Local authority services

Meet the local authority ESL coordinator. If there is a central ESL welcome centre for your local authority, visit it and introduce yourself to the staff. Identify local authority resources for translators, interpreters and settlement agencies.

School services

Review your school office routines for registration and documentation of new pupils. Meet with the school ESL/ESOL teacher or coordinator regularly:

- Clarify your relative roles and responsibilities.
- Agree on a tracking system for documentation, including registration, assessment and placement. Involve your office coordinator in this discussion.

Meet with all ESL/ESOL teachers and educational assistants for an overview of the programmes and services in the school. Look for links between ESL/ESOL staff and programmes and other school staff and programmes; for example, the mainstream curriculum, special education programme and guidance services.

Relationships

Build positive relationships with all ESL/ESOL pupils, parents and staff. Manage the expectations of staff and parents of ESL/ESOL pupils. Enlist the support of local authority resources to ensure that all procedures are culturally appropriate.

Visiting staff

Consult with any visiting ESL/ESOL teachers, liaison officers, or translators assigned to your school:

- Clarify relative roles and responsibilities.
- Review where visiting staff work while at the school. Ensure that they have appropriate space to meet with pupils, parents and staff. Balance privacy with pupil protection.
- Inform visiting staff about events at the school: send them the school newsletter, invite them to staff meetings and staff get-togethers, assign mailboxes, include them in electronic staff conferences, and invite them to make presentations to staff and parents.
- Ensure that visiting staff understand their reporting duties.
- Create a list of local community support services: agencies, advocates and associations related to various issues concerning new and various cultural communities.

ESL/ESOL pupils

- Review the pupil records of all ESL/ESOL pupils.
- Determine how many pupils speak each of the first languages represented at the school.
- Review the list of all ESL/ESOL pupils in school.
- Determine what percentage of the pupil population speaks English as a second language, and collect and interpret other appropriate data.

Monitoring

Get to know ESL/ESOL pupils as individuals if possible. Attend case conferences and parent interviews for individual pupils as appropriate. Track the progress of ESL/ESOL pupils. Monitor the delivery of in-class programme modifications for ESOL pupils.

Professional development

Provide professional development activities to meet identified needs of ESL/ESOL staff. Arrange for staff to visit the local authority's ESL reception centre and ESL programmes in other schools. Provide all staff members (teaching and non-teaching) with professional learning opportunities focusing on equity, diversity and inclusion. Invite members of various ethnic communities to brief you and the staff on relevant issues.

Visit other schools yourself to observe classes and talk with headteachers about ESL/ESOL issues.

Outreach

Look for ways to welcome parents who do not speak English. Host special parent nights using simultaneous interpretation. Translate key school communications into the main languages spoken by parents. Find out if the local authority or community can help with these translations. Reflect the cultural diversity of the school throughout curriculum provision.

Monitor and implement local authority policy on inclusion throughout the school.

SCHOOL CURRICULUM 🕸 133

BE PREPARED
Manage time wisely to allow for the multitude of tasks that present themselves. Don't take on too many priorities at once. Start things on time, don't punish the punctual!

16 Special Educational Needs (SEN) and Disability

At a glance

- Definitions
- Special educational needs and disability
- Roles and responsibilities
- Assessment

Definitions

Children have special educational needs (SEN) if they have a learning difficulty which calls for special educational provision to be made for them.

Children have a *learning difficulty* if they:

a) have a significantly greater difficulty in learning than the majority of children of the same age or

b) have a disability which prevents or hinders them from making use of educational facilities of a kind generally provided for children of the same age in schools within the area of the local authority.

(Section 312, Education Act 1996)

A person has a disability if he or she has a *physical or mental impairment* that has a substantial and long-term adverse effect on his or her ability to carry out normal day-to-day activities.

(Section 1(1), Disability Discrimination Act 1995)

Physical or mental impairment includes sensory impairments and also hidden impairments (for example, mental illness or mental health problems, learning difficulties, dyslexia and conditions such as diabetes or epilepsy).

(Disability Rights Commission Code of Practice for Schools (2002), 4.3)

⮩ Special educational needs and disability

1. *SEN Code of Practice*, November 2001

(a) Terminology
This is the revised version of the first *SEN Code of Practice* published in 1994 and takes account of SEN provisions in the Special Educational Needs and Disability Act 2001 (often referred to as SENDA).

Although there is a lack of clarity about the terms 'SEN' and 'disability', increasingly they are being used together.

The revised *SEN Code of Practice* recognizes four main types of SEN:

- communication and interaction
- cognition and learning
- behaviour, social and emotional development
- sensory and/or physical needs.

There is also a mention of *medical conditions*:

> A medical diagnosis or disability does not necessarily imply SEN … Some pupils may not require statements or school-based SEN provision, but they have medical conditions that, if not properly managed, could hinder their access to education.
>
> (p. 88, para. 7.64)

(b) The SEN coordinator (SENCO)
The headteacher needs to ensure that someone is carrying out this important role. The responsibilities will vary with the size of the school. In small schools, it may be the headteacher who takes on this role. In larger schools, SENCOs will be heading up a team of staff who are working with pupils who have SEN. (For further details, see below: Roles and responsibilities, 3.)

(c) Levels of support for SEN
The *SEN Code of Practice* recommends 'graduated response' when a pupil has been identified as having SEN:

- *School Action*   This is the first level of response. If a child is making little progress, or is demonstrating problems under any of the four headings given previously, (see above: 1(a) Terminology), then action must be taken by the class or subject teacher, to enable the pupil to learn more effectively. The SENCO will be involved in helping the teacher(s) to write an 'Individual Education Plan' (IEP). This will set targets for the child to achieve and specify the additional resources that will be used to help the child reach them.

- *School Action Plus*   If the pupil fails to make adequate progress, the SENCO will increase the level of support by placing the pupil on the next level. This means that the school will look beyond its own resources to address the pupil's needs. This might be local authority support and/or advisory services, an outreach teacher from a special school, or some other external agency. The IEP will be updated with the help of the additional staff involved. If the pupil still fails to make satisfactory progress, the school can request a statutory assessment (see the section below on Assessment).

2.   Code of Practice for Schools (July 2002)

This code of practice, published by the Disability Rights Commission (DRC), is based on Part 4 of the Disability Discrimination Act (DDA) 1995, as amended by the Special Educational Needs and Disability Act (SENDA) 2001.

The code explains the duties placed on schools by these Acts and illustrates these duties through examples. Further information is given in the next section.

During 2006, the DRC will be issuing guidance on a new requirement known as the *Disability Equality Duty*. By December 2006, secondary schools in England must have a *Disability Equality Scheme*, the deadline for Wales is April 2007 and December 2007 for primary schools in England.

Roles and responsibilities

1.   The governing body

Under the 1996 Educational Act, the governing body is responsible for:

- deciding with the headteacher the school's SEN Policy; this must be monitored and kept under review
- doing its best to ensure that the necessary provision is made for any pupils who have SEN
- making every effort to see that any special arrangements are in place, that parents are kept informed of these and that staff are aware of the pupils' needs

- making sure teachers are aware of the need to identify pupils and teach them appropriately
- making arrangements for all pupils, including those with SEN, to be able to join in the activities offered by the school as far as is practical.

Under the Disability Discrimination Act (1995) the governing body is responsible for not unlawfully discriminating against a disabled child. This includes:

- treating a disabled pupil less favourably for a reason relating to his or her disability
- failing to take reasonable steps to ensure that disabled pupils are not placed at a substantial disadvantage, in comparison with their non-disabled peers, without justification (this is known as the 'reasonable adjustments duty')
- developing an accessibility plan showing how, over time, the school will plan to increase access for pupils, prospective pupils and other users. As well as access for the physically disabled, the plan needs to consider increasing access for other types of disability as well. The first of these three-year plans ran from April 2003 to March 2006.

2. The headteacher

Headteachers are automatically members of the governing body and remain as such unless they choose not to be. It is often the case that this facilitates close working relationships between the headteacher and the governing body.

It is important to clarify who is going to take responsibility for the actual production of the SEN Policy and the Accessibility Plan, as these are very important documents.

If the headteacher is not doubling up as the SENCO, she or he must ensure that a suitable appointment is made. This would normally be a qualified teacher, although, in the wake of Workforce Remodelling, some schools are appointing people without Qualified Teacher Status (QTS). This needs careful consideration in the light of the duties expected from the SENCO.

While the SENCO will be responsible for the day-to-day management of pupils with SEN and their provision, the headteacher will need to be the link with the governors in ensuring that everything is in place and running efficiently.

3.   The special educational needs coordinator (SENCO)

Regardless of the size of the school, the responsibilities are similar. They include:

- overseeing the implementation of the SEN Policy
- coordinating the support for pupils with SEN
- managing the staff (this may include teachers and teaching assistants) who are supporting pupils with SEN
- being responsible for the record-keeping associated with pupils who have SEN
- contributing to the professional development of staff in the field of SEN
- liaising with external agencies and with parents.

4.   Other staff

Despite the fact that the governors, the headteacher and the SENCO have very specific roles, it is important that the headteacher makes sure that all staff see it as part of their responsibilities to be concerned with the welfare and progress of all the pupils for whom they have some responsibility. The role of the SENCO is to give extra support to other staff, not to remove responsibility from them for the pupils they teach.

5.   The local authority/children's service

Local authorities have a general duty to ensure that pupils with SEN are admitted to a mainsteam school, if that is what the parents want, provided that the child's inclusion is not incompatible with the efficient education of the other pupils. The local authority must consult a mainsteam school before naming it on a statement and the school must be sent a copy of that statement.

Assessment

As well as the tests that are taken by all pupils, it is essential to record the progress of pupils with SEN from the start, in order to monitor their progress, or lack of it.

1. Baseline assessment

The evidence collected on a child who is being placed on 'School Action' should be specific enough to serve as a starting point from which to measure future progress. It will also inform the development of an IEP.

2. School Action and School Action Plus

Individual Education Plans should be reviewed every six months, termly or more frequently, depending on the age of the child and the nature of his or her difficulties. A record will be kept of when targets are met and new ones set. This will help to indicate progress. Indeed, a lack of progress is likely to be the reason from moving a child from School Action to School Action Plus.

3. Statutory assessment

If, despite the school's best efforts, assisted by external agencies, progress remains very limited, the school, the parents or other agencies may decide to request the local authority to carry out a statutory assessment. This involves LA consideration of whether or not this appears to be necessary. If, after consulting with the school, the parents and other agencies, it decides to go ahead, the LA must seek in writing:

- parental views
- educational views
- medical views
- psychological views
- social services views
- any other views (including the child's wishes, if appropriate).

This is standard practice, even if, for instance, there has been no contact with social services.

When all the advice has been received, the LA decides whether or not to issue a statement.

4. Statementing

A statement is used if 'It is necessary for the LA to determine the special educational provision which the child's learning difficulty calls for' (Education Act 1996, Section 324(1)).

A statement must be issued if the child is being moved to a special school, but over half the statements are given to pupils remaining in mainstream schools.

There are six parts to a statement:

- Part 1   The details of the child and family
- Part 2   A description of the child's SEN
- Part 3   The provision that is needed
- Part 4   The type and name of school to meet the identified needs
- Part 5   Any non-educational needs
- Part 6   Any non-educational provision.

There are strict time limits for issuing a statement (see the *SEN Code of Practice*, ch. 8). An annual review must be held of any child who has a statement.

5.   The SEN and Disability Tribunal (SENDIST)

Parents have the right to appeal to SENDIST if the LA refuses a request for a statutory assessment, or if they are unhappy with the wording of the statement. The SENDIST also hears claims to do with unlawful discrimination with regard to admissions and exclusions.

17 Data-driven School Improvement

The overall objective of school improvement planning is to enhance learning and raise standards of achievement and attainment.

'Data only becomes effective when it stimulates questions about the learning needs of pupils and how these can be met. That means taking action based on objective evidence to personalise learning and maximise the progress that can be made by each child.'
(Ruth Kelly, Former Secretary of State, Education and Skills)

Getting started

1. Submit all statutory assessment to the local authority.
2. Work with the leadership team to carry out error analysis of standard assessment tasks (SATs), optional tests and any other internal assessments to identify strengths and weaknesses.
3. Evaluate the impact on achievement and attainment of the previous year's improvement plan.

4. The Performance and Assessment document (PANDA) provides a profile of the school and should be used in discussions with the leadership team and the governing body. Particular attention should be paid to:

   (a) the *contextual value added* (CVA) score (the progress made by pupils based on prior attainment taking account of a range of pupil characteristics) and

   (b) the measure of *relative attainment* in comparison with schools nationally.

5. Share the outcomes with the school leadership team and the governing body.
6. Use the findings of data analysis to identify areas for improvement.

Effective school improvement planning

The most recent Ofsted report, reports from the local authority and the school improvement partner (SIP), together with the outcomes of school self-evaluation and data analysis, will all help to form a picture of what needs to be done to bring about further improvement.

In planning for improvement, schools should be realistic in what can be achieved in one year and should not focus on too many areas at once lest it spreads its resources and efforts too thinly. The emphasis should always be on what will lead to the greatest improvement in pupils' learning.

An example of improvement planning:

To improve boys' writing
Target: —% of boys in Year— will achieve a minimum increase of — Average Points by the end of the school year.

Actions	Person responsible	Deadline	Success criteria	Monitoring	Cost	Evaluation

The role of the headteacher in improvement planning

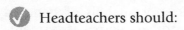 Headteachers should:

- provide the school community with the school profile detailing the nature and characteristics of the school

- involve members of the school community in school self-evaluation processes
- consult with members of the leadership team and relevant member of the governing body to identify the most significant areas for improvement
- agree with the governing body available funding to support the plan
- ensure that everyone involved in the process is clear about roles and responsibilities
- clearly explain the school improvement process to the governing body, parents and other members of the community
- arrange for appropriate professional development for staff
- ensure systems are in place to track pupils' progress (see below).
- ensure that progress is monitored and that the information is used by the leadership team in regular discussions with teachers and support staff
- ensure that planning is adjusted accordingly and that appropriate intervention is provided to support pupils.
- lead the school in celebrating success.

Tracking pupils' progress

Various commercial programmes are available to help with tracking pupils' progress, although the Department for Education and Skills (DfES) provides all schools with the Pupil Achievement Tracker (PAT) which can be downloaded from http://www.standards.dfes.gov.uk/performance/pat/FullPAT download/? version1.

It should be noted, however, that this tool, together with the PANDA, will be replaced in the autumn term 2006 by RAISEonline (Reporting and Analysis for Improvement through School Self-Evaluation). For further information about RAISEonline go to http://www.ofsted.gov.uk/schools/dataandinformationsystems.cfm.

For the RAISEonline site go to: https://www.raiseonline.org/login.aspx? Return Url=%2findex.aspx.

Other useful websites and tools to support school improvement

http://matrix.becta.org.uk
www.supportingselfevaluation.org.uk/

18 Staff Supervision and Performance Management

→ Getting started

1. Definitions and documents

Supervision refers to monitoring standards of performance and behaviour and, where necessary, applying procedures to remedy inadequate performance or improper behaviour.

Performance management refers to the evaluation of a teacher's professional practice on an annual basis.

Follow your governing body policies and procedures regarding the supervision and performance management of staff in all employee groups. These personnel procedures might include the following topics:

- performance management policies
- professional capability procedures
- ill health capability procedures

- misconduct procedures
- harassment or bullying allegations
- whistle-blowing, discrimination or grievance procedures
- dealing with child protection allegations.

All procedures will need to apply, respectively, to teaching staff and to non-teaching staff. The governing body is the employing body for the ultimate purposes of these personnel policies and procedures. The governing body will take final decisions.

Follow the steps outlined in your governing body's procedure regarding staff supervision and performance management. Acquaint yourself in some detail with the rationale behind each policy and the various 'triggers' for action.

2. The staff handbook/personnel guidance document

Determine the expectations set out in these documents for each employee group before commencing a personnel procedure or performance management process (for example, the staff handbook might specify the circumstances in which compassionate leave might be granted). Always refer to the School Teachers' Pay and Conditions Document when considering personnel/performance issues with teachers.

3. Past school practice

Discuss with senior staff:

- the history of current issues and practices at the school
- expectations concerning the respective responsibilities of line managers/responsible post-holders
- staff supervision and performance management schedules
- past performance management of individual staff members (confidentially between the headteacher and the line manager).

4. Update staff

Ensure that all staff members have a copy of performance management procedures and access to personnel policies and procedures. Arrange an occasional session for staff members who wish to discuss the procedures.

Keep yourself up to date regarding standards for teacher performance management – refer to *Regulations and Guidance for Teacher Performance Management* (DfES), the Ofsted Framework and the Professional Standards documentation.

When conducting teacher performance management, be sure to follow your governing body's policies and procedures, and the primary legislation laid down in Acts of Parliament and statutory instruments.

5. Prepare yourself

Review your governing body's expectations for your role in the supervision and performance management of:

- administrative staff
- technicians, for example, the library technician, the computer technician
- site staff
- learning support assistants, mentors
- cleaning and catering staff.

Consider the structure for line management of staff, for performance management purposes. Should anyone be performance management reviewer for more than four members of staff?

Relate whole-school and team issues to the individual performance management of staff: for example, pupil achievement, use of ICT, or community links.

◉ Supervision of deputy and assistant headteachers

What constitutes appropriate supervision of a deputy or assistant headteacher? In the absence of the headteacher, the deputy headteacher is in charge of the school and performs the duties of the headteacher. A headteacher generally supervises the deputy/assistant headteacher, and failure to do so adequately may constitute professional misconduct. Where a headteacher delegates any supervisory responsibilities to a deputy, the following actions are recommended:

- Establish an open-door policy.
- Implement a regular reporting structure on the subject matter of the delegation.
- Communicate frequently and regularly about 'problem' pupils, staff and other issues.

- Ensure that any reporting mechanisms put in place are utilized according to the stated intention.
- Advise all staff of the headteacher's ultimate responsibility for any and all problems, such as that serious issues should also be reported directly to the headteacher regardless of any general delegation of authority (see section on delegation).

Staff supervision and performance management

Visitors and volunteers

As these are not employees, the powers of headteachers to supervise, that is, to require appropriate behaviour and standards from visitors and volunteers is limited to:

a) clear statements of what is required; and
b) removal of the volunteer status and removal of visitors from the site in extreme cases.

Staff misconduct and staff capability

Discipline matters/misconduct is where staff disobey a reasonable instruction or choose to behave in an inappropriate manner.
Capability is where a staff member is unable through reasons of health, aptitude, ability, experience or training to deliver satisfactory standards.

1. Discipline matters/misconduct
Always consult with your local authority (LA) personnel department or your human resources (HR) bureau/service before taking disciplinary action. A proper misconduct procedure may result in the following sanctions:

- first or minor offence – oral warning
- serious or repeated offence – written warning; letter of reprimand
- very serious – final written warning
- gross misconduct – dismissal with or without notice.

These sanctions are not tied directly to any particular 'level' of offence. Each discipline situation must be considered on its own merits. If there are repeated incidents of the same behaviour, the consequences may escalate accordingly. Disciplinary allegations are dealt with in a hearing to which the staff member is invited.

The staff member is advised of the right to representation, in advance, and will need to be given an adequate opportunity to defend him or herself and answer the allegations.

Ensure that you follow your local authority/school policy and procedures.

2. Written warnings

This would be a letter containing:

- a description of the unacceptable behaviour
- a statement of expected behaviour
- consequences for noncompliance up to and including dismissal.

3. Inappropriate or unacceptable behaviour

Situations of inappropriate or unacceptable behaviour arise when staff violate – through their behaviour – the reasonable instructions provided by the head-teacher or some other authorized senior person. Such behaviour may arise when a staff member carries out an action which is clearly unprofessional, dangerous, unacceptable, injurious, or otherwise intolerable – even if no actual instruction has been given, for example, racist behaviour, violence, theft, fraud, harassment, and so on.

Such situations include but are not limited to:

- failure to follow a reasonable instruction by management
- inappropriate language
- inappropriate actions
- racial or sexual harassment of colleagues or pupils or other human rights violations
- chronic lateness with no satisfactory explanation
- disclosing confidential information
- unauthorized absence
- refusal to plan, deliver or follow up lessons, reports, meetings, consultations, and so on
- pursuing an inappropriate relationship with a pupil
- criminal activity
- refusal to accept the authority of management to manage, that is, insubordination
- other behaviour generally considered professionally unacceptable.

Incidents of inappropriate or unacceptable behaviour are dealt with through the disciplinary process.

4. Capability issues

If a member of staff appears to be willing but unable to deliver satisfactory standards of performance, then their capability is put in question. This means that they may not have the skill, aptitude, ability, experience or training to reach the required standard. If the work expected of him or her is indeed appropriate in your view, then the premise under which 'capability procedures' will operate is that they can and will become capable of delivering satisfactory quality performance.

What will be needed is

- a clear statement of the standards
- evidence that there is a significant failure
- extra support, coaching, training resources and any other reasonable provision to give the member of staff the chance to improve.

This support may, initially, be informal. If progress is not made then headteachers will have to seriously consider moving into the official personnel procedure for capability. If, after a series of review meetings, it is still obvious that a satisfactory standard is not being met, then the governing body will need to consider termination of the employment.

5. Local authority support

For community schools and others that use LA personnel or HR services, the headteacher will be entitled to ongoing support in managing a misconduct procedure or a capability procedure. Human Resources staff should accompany the headteacher at hearings or review meetings or when presenting a management case to governors. Any governing body panel which meets to consider a dismissal or an appeal should also be entitled to the services of an HR adviser.

6. Staff taking out a grievance

Personnel procedures for capability, misconduct, performance management or other staffing issues usually build in the right of appeal to a governing body appeal panel by the 'accused' who wishes to challenge the headteacher's position as regards procedure, verdict, decision or sanction.

In other cases not directly related to the progress of a personnel 'case' the headteacher may find him or herself the subject of a grievance by the member of staff. The headteacher will need to justify their position: explaining to a grievance panel of governors what they did and why.

The application of reasonable professional judgement, supported by evidence should ensure a grievance is dismissed.

Advice from your professional association is always available in these situations. Staff taking out a grievance or lodging an appeal are likely to enlist the support of their union, whose representative may challenge the headteacher's professional judgement or practice.

Remember, just because other staff do not like your decisions or do not agree with your decisions does not mean that your decisions are wrong.

BE VISIBLE

Take time to stay connected to pupils and staff. That is why you are a headteacher.
Visit a classroom every day.
Be in the hall when classes change and they will think you are everywhere.

19 Staff Selection and Development

Staff selection: getting started

One of the most significant and rewarding aspects of your job as a head-teacher is the recruitment, selection and development of new staff.

1. The governing body selection and recruitment policy should state what role members of the governing body should play in the selection and recruitment of new staff. It should also state what the role of the head-teacher, or indeed any other senior post-holder who may become involved in appointments, will be.
2. The local authority human resources team or the school's HR bureau/provider (if it is not the local authority) will be able to advise the school governors and the headteacher about best practice as regards advertising, long-listing, short-listing, references, person specifications, job descriptions and selection procedures.

3. The DfES document, *Safeguarding Children: Safer Recruitment and Selection in Education Settings*, published in 2005, emphasizes the importance of developing measures to deter, identify and reject people who might abuse children or who are otherwise unsuited to work with them. It provides guidance to be used in recruitment and selection procedures and other Human Resources management processes.

4. Although an enhanced disclosure will be required from the Criminal Records Bureau (CRB) for any staff who are going to work with children, the disclosure does not give a headteacher or governing body definitive answers as to whether a person should be employed. There is still scope for discretion and judgement if a candidate has a 'record', on his/her disclosure, of criminal convictions or cautions, or some details on his/her disclosure of unproven, false or malicious allegations. The more recent and the more condemnatory the disclosure records, the less likely it is that it will be safe to employ the candidate.

5. Some candidates from overseas or with a less than complete career record may not be able to provide full disclosures: such applications may be entirely genuine and be from good candidates. Advice needs to be sought from the local authority concerning qualifications, qualified teacher status, and so on.

6. Candidates are entitled to expect that the prospective employer operates fairly and that the recruitment process is seen to be non-discriminatory; gender, race, disability, sexual orientation, age and religious affiliation should not feature in a discriminating way.

7. Build a relationship with your personnel officer who is responsible for staffing and recruitment advice.

8. The principles applying to the selection and recruitment of teaching and support staff are, in the main, similar.

Selection procedures

The governing body selection policy will indicate what delegated committee of staff and governors is charged with the responsibility of managing the selection process, and to what extent the selection committee has delegated executive powers to decide on a successful candidate and to require the local authority to employ the candidate. Although a local authority may wish to advise the committee on the most suitable candidate, the committee will make the final decision, which can be challenged by the local authority only on technical grounds, that is that the candidate is not appropriately qualified, is on List 99 or has some other legally prohibiting condition.

The candidate profile

- The committee will determine the profile, or person specification, for the post indicating:

  - qualifications required
  - experience expected
  - personal characteristics that are preferable
  - the skill, aptitude and ability mix that the ideal candidate might offer.

- The committee will also examine the job description for the post and clarify the roles and responsibilities of the post-holder.
- When advertising the vacancy, the person specification, job description, salary and contractual aspects, details of the school and wider community, and the selection arrangements should all be clearly described.
- The advertisement should make clear the organization's commitment to safeguarding and promoting the welfare of children, and that recruitment procedures will involve obtaining and scrutinizing comprehensive information from applicants, including satisfactorily resolving any discrepancies or anomalies.
  These procedures will include

  - obtaining references
  - an interview
  - verification of the applicant's identity
  - verification of the applicant's qualifications and experience
  - verification of health and physical capability
  - criminal records/List 99 checks.

- References should be obtained on short-listed candidates before interview.
- The committee should make it clear to candidates how the various elements of the person specification are to be assessed during the selection process, that is, via:

  - references
  - application form
  - health checks/questionnaires/occupational health referral
  - CRB/police/List 99 checks
  - presentations to a panel
  - in-tray exercises

- practical demonstration of teaching skills
- preliminary and final interviews, and so on.

There should be a scoring or assessment system in place whereby each aspect of the person specification is graded for each candidate: the committee/panel's job will be to score or assess each aspect of the specification. It will normally be expected that the candidate who scores the highest total is offered the post.

- Papers and records of the selection process should be kept safely for some time, to provide evidence of impartiality and objectivity if there is a retrospective accusation of bias or discrimination by an unsuccessful candidate.
- Questions in an interview can include asking about:

  - motivational aspects – 'What drives you on in this work?'
  - relationships aspects – 'How do you get on with (adults/pupils)?'
  - emotional resilience – 'How do you cope with challenges, tensions or conflicts?'

- It should be clear which panel/committee members ask which questions. It is helpful to have a standard initial list of questions common to all candidates, but a follow-up question, probing an initial answer, may well be quite individual.
- Timing of interviews is crucial – they should be thorough without being exhausting.

  - Build in comfort breaks.
  - Stick to the timetable so that candidates can prepare/relax and so on.

- If no candidate emerges that fulfils the basic requirements of the post it is usually better to re-advertise and postpone selection rather than employing a person who fails to meet the criteria in full.
- It may be helpful to ask each candidate, 'If you were to be offered the post would you be likely to accept it?' This will reduce the likelihood of your preferred candidate actually turning you down: it does happen.

Successful candidates may sometimes ask for time to consider: it is up to the panel/committee as to whether to allow perhaps 24 hours or to ask for an immediate decision.

- Notify unsuccessful candidates as quickly as possible; offer verbal and/or written feedback to unsuccessful candidates but:

- be brief and factual
- do not insist if they do not want any feedback
- do not discuss the merits of other candidates, merely how the individual measured up to the person specification.

- Welcome new staff, when all post-offer checks are complete and the appointment is confirmed. Make any announcements, invite new appointees in for a visit, and start discussing arrangements for induction and probation.
- If there is only one candidate then all of the above should be properly carried out; the decision will be whether the one candidate meets all the required criteria.

> Effective headteachers hire and retain high-quality teachers and hold them responsible for pupil learning.

➔ Teaching staff development: getting started

> **TIP**
>
> Staff development, professional development, professional growth, professional learning: the ultimate goal of all of these is to improve teaching and thus improve pupil achievement.

As headteacher, your staff development role at the school, which may be delegated to a continuous professional development (CPD) coordinator, has many facets, including:

- working with staff to identify their professional needs reflecting relevant national standards
- planning, organizing and facilitating staff development programmes that improve staff effectiveness and are consistent with school goals and needs
- supervising both individuals and groups
- providing feedback on performance
- arranging for support and assistance for individuals as needed
- engaging staff and others to plan and participate in staff development activities
- initiating your own professional development.

Source: Thompson, 1993, pp. 11–13.

1.   School staff development plan – the professional development plan

Review the following:

- school strategic plan (improvement plan)
- human resources policies and procedures relating to staff development
- local authority handbook on staff management and professional development
- school's staff development plan (update in consultation with staff)
- relevant collective agreement clauses.

The staff development plan should include the following:

- an overall focus relating to school improvement priorities, significant goals and specific objectives
- responsibility holders and timelines
- strategies to encourage staff participation
- resources available, including time and money
- a list (and schedule) of planned staff development activities
- supports available as follow-up to these activities (for example, mentoring and coaching)
- a process to assess the results and impact of the staff development activities
- a procedure for evaluating and modifying the staff development plan itself.

The staff development plan will be linked to the data-driven school improvement plan and local authority strategic plans, and should address such topics as:

- curriculum knowledge
- pupil assessment
- special education
- teaching strategies
- classroom management and leadership
- use of technology
- communicating with parents and students.

2.   Local authority and external resources

Find out which local authority personnel are responsible for staff development and curriculum support. Introduce yourself and find out how they can assist you with the staff development programme at your school. Get a copy of the local authority's professional development calendar. Apprise yourself of professional development projects that may be available through the local university, college, the National College for School Leadership (NCSL) or professional association.

3. Staff participation

Invite teachers at the school to make presentations to staff on topics of interest to peers. Look for ways to provide presenters with time to prepare. Seek input from staff as to the best format, location and time for these sessions.

Consider a staff development component for staff meetings. These regular presentations can be given by invited guests, staff members or representatives from the local authority. Be sure to prepare and present some of these staff development sessions yourself.

Consult staff on how to make best use of in-school professional activity days.

4. New staff

Provide induction programmes for all new staff members, including newly qualified and experienced teachers and non-teaching staff.

Provide new staff with a comprehensive staff handbook. Invite staff members to help update the staff handbook annually. This is an excellent professional development opportunity for interested individuals.

Develop an ongoing plan for supporting recently qualified teachers. This might include:

- regular information and discussion sessions dealing with anticipated activities (for example, the first day of school, parent–teacher interviews, completing reports, developing professional learning plans and portfolios)
- individual coaching for each newly qualified teacher through a mentoring relationship with an experienced teacher in the school (see below for further information)
- mentor teachers who are interested in further career development beyond the classroom.

5. Headteacher's professional development

Be sure to develop your own professional learning plan for the year; do not neglect yourself. Share your personal plan with the staff; model your commitment to lifelong learning.

Establish a mentoring relationship for yourself with a more experienced headteacher. Get involved in professional associations locally and nationally.

Take advantage of training and information opportunities provided by your local authority and by the National College for School Leaders. Remember, you cannot be an expert in everything all at once. Set a focus for yourself and establish your priorities over a three- to five-year cycle.

See Part V, 'Looking After Yourself', for more suggestions concerning your own professional development.

> Effective headteachers provide opportunities for teachers to work, plan and think together:
>
> - Common planning: time and space is set aside for teachers to work together
> - Subject area or National Curriculum area meetings: effective headteachers participate in these meetings
> - Coaching and mentoring: expert teachers coach new teachers; individuals work with mentors.
>
> (National Association of Elementary School Principals, 2001, pp. 45–50)

Professional learning

Further opportunities for professional growth: an overview

Support and encourage staff members as they plan and undertake a variety of professional learning activities. The following is an overview of a wide variety of opportunities available to teachers.

Accredited study opportunities.
Academic programmes including degree and postgraduate work:

- Universities and colleges.

Professional networks:

- Participate in subject councils.
- Work within school and advisory and development groups.
- Join informal study or reading groups.

Mentoring or coaching:

- Engage in paired teaching and observation.
- Mentor a new teacher.

Learning through practice:

- Develop new curriculum materials.
- Conduct action research.
- Pilot new initiatives.

Research activities:

- Plan and conduct research.
- Explore ways to access and use educational research.

Professional activities:

- Visit other educational settings.
- Develop a reading list.
- Maintain a professional portfolio.

Professional contributions:

- Make presentations at conferences.
- Contribute to professional publications.

Technology and learning:

- Engage in professional learning using ICT.
- Research on the Internet.

Working with newly qualified or recently qualified teachers

You may have several newly qualified teachers (NQTs) on staff every year. Working with them both individually and collectively will be a very significant part of your job. Use your local authority NQT induction programme in conjunction with your school-based programme.

Invite all new staff members to visit the school for an initial orientation session. Provide all new staff with a comprehensive staff handbook. Plan induction programmes for all new staff members, including newly qualified and experienced teachers and non-teaching staff. Make sure the induction for new staff is not limited to a one-day event.

Provide for ongoing support for NQTs within your school's staff development plan. Ensure that newly qualified teachers understand the teacher performance appraisal process.

Design and deliver an induction programme to support NQTs. This programme might include:

- regular information and discussion sessions dealing with anticipated activities (for example, the first day of school, parent–teacher interviews, completing reports, developing professional INSET and portfolios)
- individual coaching for each NQT through a mentoring relationship with an experienced teacher in the school.

Let new teachers have adequate and high-quality stock and resources. Ensure that department heads and team leaders have the curriculum resources they need to support the new teachers in their departments and teams.

Take a look at new teachers' classrooms; look for an opportunity to commend.

Tell them why they need to be professional and courteous to parents, carers, visitors, representatives and other professionals. Talk to new teachers about early proactive contact with parents and the power of positive calls bringing good news.

Provide support systems for their high-profile and special needs pupils.

In the third or fourth week of September, spend some quality discussion time with new teachers to find out how their year has started. Most important, let them know that *no* question is too silly.

HIRE WELL

Staffing decisions are critical.
If I could give only one piece of advice, it would be to hire well.

20 Professional Relationships

At a glance

- Working with the unions in your school

  Managing in a union environment: an overview
  Building and maintaining positive relationships: getting started

- Possible tensions with the unions

  Personnel practices and collective agreements: getting started
  Grievances: an overview

- Official union disputes/industrial action

Working with the unions in your school

Managing in a union environment: an overview

As a headteacher or senior manager, you are no longer part of the main 'teacher' workforce; you are now part of senior leadership and as such, represent the school governors and the local authority. Your responsibility is to ensure that you operate in accordance with all provisions of the staff handbook, personnel procedures and any collective agreements for the employee groups at the school. You need to understand the detail of any collective agreements.

Teachers may be less likely to share issues and concerns with you than they were when you were a teacher, especially issues related to discontent with your management style. Your influence is through the management structure, not through any staffroom or co-union membership.

In some situations, you might be accused of unfair professional or staffing practices, for example:

- undermining legal sanctions
- using intimidation
- using threats
- using undue influence
- coercion, which can be regarded as anti-union or interfering in the membership or activities of a trade union or the representation of employees by a trade union.

As headteachers and deputy headteachers, you and your colleagues may:

- serve as management representatives on union–management committees
- participate in district meetings and district committee meetings without obligations to unions
- supervise and discipline staff solely from a management perspective
- be involved in tasks on behalf of senior management
- have significant increases in responsibilities.

Building and maintaining positive relationships: getting started

1.   Treat the unions with respect

- Invite the staff members to elect/nominate a school representative from each union on site.
- Invite union representatives to provide items for the staff meeting agenda and joint committees.
- Respect unions and their rights under collective agreements, which will have been formally agreed with the employer/local authority.
- Invite union representation to attend meetings with individual staff members when discipline or capability procedures are contemplated. However, there is no absolute right for a member of staff to be accompanied by a union representative, except where provided in a procedure being followed.
- Understand the role of the union representatives and branch officials and facilitate their roles; for example, support collective agreement provisions for time off to conduct union business, subject to the need to leave lesson plans for classes.
- Do not personalize collective agreement disputes, especially grievances.

2. Recognize that you are part of the management team

- Be professional and collaborative with those you supervise.
- Understand the significance of personnel procedures as a reserve position, if staff are unable or unwilling to work to an acceptable professional standard.
- Support management's perspective in union-orientated discussions (unless of course, your own position needs union support because it is under threat).
- Find out which of your colleagues, and which local authority employees, have expertise to offer in the area of union relations; know when to seek their advice and assistance.

3. Continue to work toward developing a collaborative culture with staff

- Explain to the school staff that the professional requirements to fulfil obligations to Ofsted, the local authority, the DfES, the governing body, the *Every Child Matters* agenda and the local community require continuous attention and a team approach.
- Continue to solicit staff input and feedback.
- Take training in problem-solving, conflict resolution negotiation and political management.

> The entire school staff is interdependent. Its members must rely on each other and be able to resolve their differences.
> There are too many pressures on educators today to allow staff–headteacher conflict to erode the professional harmony that is a basic necessity in every effective school.

→ Possible tensions with the unions

Personnel practices and collective agreements: getting started

1. *Identify* which unions operate in your school. Meet with the union representatives in your school. Invite them to brief you. Find out who the local officers are for your local authority. Record their names and telephone numbers. Introduce yourself.
2. *Review* current copies of any collective agreement(s) in force in your school. Check how and when they were agreed, and with whom. Confirm the role of the local authority in these agreements. Check if they

are current, and liaise with your fellow headteachers in the area to ascertain how significant they are. Personnel practices clarify recommended actions for school staff and management in an effort to promote fairness and consistency. Staff handbook details usually address matters that include the following:

(a) salary, pay policy, performance management and expenses
(b) responsibility allowances, threshold, and other remuneration matters
(c) holiday entitlement and compassionate leave
(d) benefits and gratuities
(e) staffing and staffing committees
(f) line management reporting arrangements
(g) working conditions (for example, allocation of teaching and preparation time, protocols for supervision of pupils' health and safety)
(h) staff evaluation and monitoring
(i) grievances and complaints.

Grievances: an overview

Grievances are generally defined as concerns, problems or complaints that employees raise with their employers. Grievances are sometimes brought forward by their union on behalf of their members. Issues that may cause grievances include:

- terms and conditions of employment
- health and safety
- work relations
- bullying and harassment
- new working practices
- working environment
- organizational change
- equal opportunities.

The grievance procedure usually includes a number of defined steps:

1. Informal discussion with line manager. This may also include mediation between aggrieved parties.
2. Formal stage, which will clarify the grievance, articulating clearly the actions or incidents that are the subject of the grievance, giving reasons why the actions are thought to be inappropriate and any evidence that

may support the concerns and the outcomes that are requested if the grievance is upheld.

3. Appeal involving a panel of governors to review the decision made at the previous stage.

Most grievance policies will ensure that the process ends following appeal stage; there should be no further referral to local authority, diocese or other body.

Check the grievance procedure adopted by your governing body for each specific grievance. It is crucial that the procedure is followed, in particular any timelines must be adhered to.

Discuss the situation with your local authority personnel provider if you believe you are in a grievance situation. Be wary of discussing too much detail with governors as they need to remain neutral, in case they are needed subsequently as panel members.

Strategies to assist headteachers with union disputes and grievances

Be fair and reasonable. Be aware that your actions and decisions can be challenged.

Recognize the professional experience to be gained through challenges and second opinions.

Document; maintain confidential files securely.

Take advice regarding grievance/staffing issues, for example from the local authority and human resources department, first.

Official union disputes/industrial action

An official union-backed dispute and/or industrial action does happen from time to time in schools and colleges.

*   There are various legal stages that the union members will have to go through in terms of union notices, indicative ballots and so on before staff members will gain union protection if they are considering taking industrial action.
*   Any official dispute will be with the employer: the local authority or governing body. Headteachers and senior staff are employees and are therefore not the target of the dispute.

- The role of headteachers will be to follow the direct instruction of their employer in terms of directions to staff, to report to the employer any information they have about the actions of staff members, and to manage the school on an operational basis as safely and effectively as possible given that some staff may not be working during a dispute.
- Headteachers and senior staff should not take sides or lobby for one cause or another, because headteachers have to work with all sectors of the school community after the dispute has resolved.
- Headteachers should not strike-break by covering work normally done by others, but can make alternative staffing arrangement under the employer's direction, as they would if an employee was absent through illness.
- Health and safety considerations are paramount – if aspects of the school's activity are not safe then they must be abandoned.

BE PREPARED

Read and understand the collective agreements.
Keep organized records securely.
Rely on evidence, not opinion.
De-personalize stressful situations.

21 Celebrating Success

→ Getting started

Effective headteachers honour and recognize those who have worked to serve pupils and the purpose of the school.

Celebrating the accomplishments of pupils, parents and staff is an important component of your role as headteacher. Celebrations are one way to foster a positive school culture – and school culture is a significant factor in pupil motivation and achievement, and in teacher work satisfaction and productivity.

Here are some suggestions for getting started.

1. Know and be able to articulate (be passionate about) your own values and beliefs about learning and teaching, and about how pupils' and teachers' achievements should be recognized and rewarded.
2. Understand and respect the traditions and history, heroes and heroines, symbols and ceremonies at your new school – 'the way we do things here'. It is important to get to know the school's culture as quickly as possible. Culture can be changed, but this usually takes time.
3. Determine whether there are identifiable subcultures or subgroups of pupils, staff and families in the school; view such diversity as an opportunity.

Shaping school culture

'It is up to school leaders – headteachers, teachers and often parents – to help identify, shape and maintain strong, positive, pupil-focused cultures.'

(Peterson and Deal, 1998, p. 28)

---

4. Assess your school against the following school culture norms, which need to be strong in order to create a healthy school:

   (a) collegiality
   (b) experimentation without blame
   (c) high expectations
   (d) trust and confidence
   (e) tangible support
   (f) reaching out to the knowledge base
   (g) appreciation and recognition
   (h) caring, celebration, and humour
   (i) involvement in decision-making
   (j) protection of what's important
   (k) traditions
   (l) honest, open communication.

Source: Saphier and King, 1984, pp. 67–74.

5. Acknowledge that there are unique cultural differences in each school. Each school will respond differently to change; staff and pupils will react differently to appreciation and recognition.
6. Help the school community focus on the pupils: begin by telling the stories (past and present) of their accomplishments and achievements.
7. Consider which policies and programmes support an emotionally healthy school.

8. Determine what elements of the culture are standing in the way of the success of pupils, staff and parents, and how to move away from those elements without alienating stakeholders.
9. Discuss your findings and observations about school culture and celebrating success with headteacher colleagues, a mentor, and the deputy headteacher and leadership team.
10. Don't try to change things too quickly at your new school. Observe, listen, and learn.

> 'Recognition is a cure for many ills.'
>
> (Kuhn and Nasar, 2001, p. vii)

Creating an environment for success

Model the behaviour you want others to exhibit

- Focus your energies on success.
- Be optimistic, respectful and thoughtful.
- Share time, skills, ideas and resources.
- Engage in conversations about teaching and learning.
- Be humble and learn from others by listening and observing.
- Ask for ideas, help and volunteers.
- Request feedback on your performance.
- Attend pupil assemblies, sporting events, concerts, dramatic presentations, and so on.
- Analyse the ways in which motivation works; talk about motivation with staff, pupils and parents.
- Encourage positive relationships and open communication with parents.

Expect the best

- Articulate clearly school standards and goals.
- Welcome staff and pupils into the building each day.
- Catch people doing something right.
- Look for examples of best practice.
- Ensure that appropriate time, support and resources are available to design and implement a ceremony or special event.
- Make role models of former pupils, community members and nationally known personalities.
- Encourage staff, pupils and parents to be proud of great work.

Design a rewards and recognition programme

- Reward pupils and staff for attaining their personal best.
- Recognize the variety of ways pupils and staff can be successful.
- Provide performance feedback on an ongoing basis.
- Look for ways to provide positive feedback to staff and pupils.
- Ensure that every pupil has at least one adult mentor in the school ... possibly the form tutor, maybe a member of the support staff.
- Honour the need for choice and control.
- Celebrate accomplishments of former pupils and staff.
- Keep a file of recognition ideas.
- Write thank you notes.
- E-mail positive comments about a classroom visit.
- Create a headteacher's recognition event honouring pupils. Have an end-of-year awards assembly.
- Have private as well as public rewards and recognition.
- Involve the governing body, pupil council and staff in designing a recognition programme.

> Keep in mind that different people react differently to public recognition. Also, be sensitive to jealousies that can arise among staff or pupils in response to public praise.

Link rewards and praise to standards and values

- Insist on courtesy and respect from staff, pupils, parents and visitors to the school.
- Phone or write to parents or guardians when a pupil has met a goal or reached a milestone.
- Ask the pupils about their learning during a classroom visit.
- Talk with the pupils about their dreams and goals.
- Acknowledge and honour existing school traditions.
- Design new traditions and ceremonies that reflect changing beliefs and values.
- Ensure celebrations reflect the traditions of all cultures and religions represented in the school community.
- Include all pupils.
- Balance competition with cooperation.
- Create opportunities for staff to get together professionally and socially.

Sharing success

Schedule celebrations

- Hold assemblies featuring pupil performances and awards.
- Host recognition events for volunteers, community helpers, sports coaches, bus drivers, 'Lollipop' people, cooks, cleaners and bottle-washers!
- Celebrate heroes and heroines whose behavior exemplifies the school's core values.
- Invite staff, parents and members of the community to challenge the pupils to a sports activity – beware the perils of too competitive or physical an activity; a parents versus pupils rugby match might be quite hazardous.
- Celebrate staff and pupil accomplishments.

> The local authority may appreciate being kept informed about the accomplishments of pupils and staff at your school. Pass along the good news.

Recognize milestones, transitions and changes

- Host a school anniversary reunion.
- Plan special events to mark a school amalgamation or relaunch.
- Take time to explain why you made certain decisions.
- Share information about local authority approaches; help pupils, staff and parents understand the requirements.
- When dealing with a tragedy, involve the local authority emergency planning and disaster management team.

Link pupils and staff with the world outside school

- Twin with another school to promote cultural understanding.
- Adopt a community service or charity.
- Design a school website.
- Promote international exchanges for both pupils and teachers.
- Invite pupils and teachers from other countries for a study or work term.
- Create a tutor or literacy programme using pupils from the local senior school or local college.

Consciously build a positive school culture

- Promote dialogue about teaching and learning.
- Provide positive feedback to staff and pupils when change occurs.
- Foster collaborative decision-making.
- Be sure to take issues of adult learning, teacher overload and staff burnout seriously.
- Ensure that staff are aware of any local authority employee assistance programme.
- Offer leadership training to pupils as well as staff.
- Invite groups of pupils to your office for conversations on topics of their choice, having working lunches with pupil representatives.
- Start small and celebrate each success.

Negative environments

Some of the indicators of a negative environment are blaming, lack of communication, impatience, a heavy reliance on rules and punishment, individualism rather than collegiality, poor behaviour and attendance rates, poor building maintenance, rising school exclusions and decreasing academic achievement.

> Some schools develop 'toxic' cultures which actively discourage efforts to improve teaching or pupil achievement.

If you find yourself in a school with a negative environment, consider the following suggestions:

1. Based on the collaborative decision-making process, develop a school improvement plan with measurable outcomes, timelines and responsibility centres.
2. Share the action plan with all the stakeholders including, on some occasions, the media.
3. Monitor the implementation of the improvement plan; give recognition, praise and support to staff, pupils and parents who are contributing to meeting the goals.
4. Evaluate and revise your plan.
5. Celebrate the success of staff, pupils, parents and community, and share that success.

Further reading regarding school culture

M. Fullan, (2001) *Leading in a Culture of Change.*

D. Golemen, R.E. Boyatzis and A. McKee, (2002) *The New Leaders.*

K. D. Peterson, and T.E. Deal (2002) *The Shaping of School Culture Fieldbook.*

VALUE STAFF

Never lose sight of the fact that you were once a teacher.

Look for lots of ways to appreciate and recognize the efforts of staff.

Look in the shadows for those efforts that often go unnoticed.

Always keep in mind that the single most important characteristic of a highly successful classroom is the high morale of the teacher.

PART 3
Behaviour and Discipline

22 Pupil Behaviour and Discipline in the School

⊃ Getting started

1. Local authority and school codes of conduct

Know the local authority's policies and procedures on behaviour and discipline and the police and local authority protocol. (See Chapter 23, 'Pupil Behaviour and Outside Agencies', for further information regarding police and school protocols.)

Review the local authority and school codes of conduct to ensure consistency.

2. Communicating expectations

Ensure that the school code of conduct is communicated to pupils and parents at the start of the school year and on an ongoing basis. Pupils and parents need to know in advance that exclusion for a fixed period or even permanently might be the consequence of serious misconduct. Discuss school codes of conduct regularly with school staff. Provide support and information to new and temporary staff. Discuss only general issues regarding student behaviour, discipline and safety at governing body meetings throughout the year; do not discuss individuals or cases. Solicit the views of the governing body regarding the local code of conduct and school policies or guidelines concerning the appropriate dress of pupils, appearance issues, personal property issues, and so on.

3. Headteacher and deputy headteacher duties

Consult with the deputy headteacher (if there is one) on student behaviour and discipline. Clarify the roles you and the deputy headteacher will assume consistent with governing body policy. Keep in mind that the headteacher is ultimately responsible for discipline. If you delegate supervisory authority to the deputy headteacher, be sure to maintain adequate communication and supervision. The following actions are recommended:

- Establish an open-door policy.
- Implement a regular reporting structure on delegated responsibilities.
- Communicate frequently and regularly about pupils, staff and other issues.
- All serious issues should be reported directly to the headteacher regardless of any general delegation of authority.

4. Shared responsibilities

Include other staff members involved in monitoring and supporting student behaviour. Involve them in discussions and role clarification. Meet with members of the special education resource team; for example, psychiatrists, social workers, and psychologists. Clarify their roles and responsibilities in working with pupils, parents and staff. Begin immediately to build positive relationships with all parents, especially those of pupils experiencing ongoing difficulty. Prepare individual behaviour support plans and pastoral support programmes for those pupils at risk of exclusion.

5. Documentation

Document factually all interviews, incidents, meetings and phone calls regarding student behaviour and discipline. Record the time, date, place, participants and what was said. File your documentation. Establish a system, electronic or otherwise, for filing notes regarding contacts with pupils and parents. Ensure that both headteacher and deputy headteacher have access to these notes and follow the same record-keeping system. Keep all records secure.

Remember that notes may be subject to scrutiny by outside agencies. Be factual.

6. Support programmes

Find out about available school programmes, preventative measures and routines that promote a safe environment and a positive atmosphere; for example:

- anger management programmes integrated into the curriculum at each year group level
- conflict resolution, peer mediation and restorative justice programmes
- strategies to improve pupils' self-esteem and social and communication skills
- programmes to encourage student participation in school activities
- early identification and intervention strategies
- counselling or mentoring for at-risk pupils.

See Chapter 24, 'Protecting our Pupils'.

☺ Governing body policies and procedures: an overview

Behaviour, discipline and safety

Follow your governing body's policies and procedures regarding student behaviour, discipline and safety. Among others, these policies and procedures might include the following titles:

- Safe Schools – security issues
- Code of Conduct – behaviour, uniform, appearance
- Pupils at Risk of Exclusion
- Pupil Exclusion and Governor Disciplinary Panels
- Critical Incident Review – evaluation of the effectiveness of the code of conduct
- Off-site Misdemeanors – the school's remit
- Substance Abuse
- Weapons
- Access Out-of-Hours – including extended schools

- Police and Local Authority Protocol
- Searching and Confiscation Protocols
- Crisis Response Plan – emergency planning
- Tragic Events Team.

Internal suspension

- As a preceding stage to moving to a fixed-term or permanent exclusion, some schools find it helpful to isolate or internally suspend a pupil for a day or even longer.
- This strategy is staff intensive as there must be adequate supervision for isolated/suspended pupils.
- The pupil's education must continue while he/she is internally suspended.
- You, as the headteacher, should not end up looking after or supervising a number of miscreants in your office, as you risk being seen as the ultimate sanction before exclusion or being used as a convenient repository by staff.
- Internal suspension may be a useful penultimate sanction for persistent and defiant refusal to abide by the agreed disciplinary code of conduct, resulting in continuing and generalized bad behaviour.
- Instances of theft, violence, illicit substances, vandalism and racism may well be so serious that they warrant an immediate move to an exclusion.

Exclusion procedures

National government (DfES) procedures regarding student exclusion may cover the following topics:

- definitions of fixed-term and permanent exclusion
- mandatory and discretionary reasons for exclusion
- procedures to follow
- moving from fixed-term to permanent exclusion
- mitigating factors
- headteacher's investigation leading to exclusion
- duration of exclusion
- notification of exclusion
- appeal against an exclusion: the five-day and 15-day triggers
- return from exclusion – re-admittance interviews
- sample notification letters to be used.

Exclusion of a pupil

A pupil may be excluded if the pupil commits any of the following infractions while he or she is at school or is engaged in a school-related activity:

1. Possessing a weapon, including possessing a firearm.
2. Using a weapon to cause or to threaten bodily harm to another person.
3. Committing physical assault on another person that causes bodily harm requiring treatment by a medical practitioner.
4. Committing sexual assault.
5. Trafficking in weapons or in illegal drugs.
6. Committing theft.
7. Giving alcohol to a minor.
8. Engaging in another activity that, under a policy of the governing body, is one for which exclusion is mandatory.

Follow the DfES policies and procedures in all matters related to exclusion.

TIP

Behaviour codes

Remember, headteachers should solicit the views of the school governing body regarding both the local code of conduct and school policies and guidelines concerning appropriate dress of pupils, and appearance issues in general.

Codes of conduct

The purpose of a code of conduct is to set the stage for managing the behaviour of all persons on school premises.

Sample code of conduct

Guiding principles

- All participants involved in the school system – pupils, parents or guardians, volunteers, teachers and other staff members – are included in this code of conduct whether they are on school property, off-site or at school-authorized events or activities.
- All members of the school community are to be treated with respect and dignity, especially persons in positions of authority.
- Responsible citizenship involves appropriate participation in the civic life of the school community. Active and engaged citizens are aware of their rights, but more importantly, they accept responsibility for protecting their rights and the rights of others.
- Members of the school community are expected to use non-violent means to resolve conflict. Physically aggressive behaviour is never a responsible way to interact with others.
- The possession, use or threatened use of any object to injure another person endangers the safety of oneself and others.
- Alcohol and illegal drugs are addictive and present a health hazard. Schools will work cooperatively with police and drug and alcohol agencies to promote prevention strategies and, where necessary, respond to school members who are in possession of, or under the influence of, alcohol or illegal drugs.
- Insults, disrespect and other hurtful acts disrupt learning and teaching in a school community. Members of the school community have a responsibility to maintain an environment where conflict and difference can be addressed in a manner characterized by respect and civility.

Dress codes

The successful enforcement of the school dress code requires both an understanding of the school and community culture and the application of common sense and sound judgement. Your parent governors will be a useful source of advice about what uniform and appearance policies will gain broad approval among the parent body.

Access to school premises

Follow the local authority's policies and procedures regarding access to school premises. There will be explicit arrangements and documentation. Always consult with the local authority when contemplating the limiting of access or issuing a banning letter. Headteachers, through the governing body, have the power to ban anyone from the school whose presence is detrimental to the good order and management of the school.

DOCUMENT

Document all conversations with parents, teachers and pupils.
Don't jump to conclusions. Check out the story with pupils and staff before making decisions. Keep written notes on all incidents.
Always document factually, objectively, dispassionately and truthfully. It will save you hours of agonizing later when you try to remember.

23 Pupil Behaviour and Outside Agencies

At a glance

- Background to government policy on improving behaviour
- National and local authority/police and school protocols
- Search and confiscation
    - *An overview*
    - *Who and why*
- The young offender: implications for the school
    - *Governance*
    - *Record-keeping*
- School attendance
    - An overview
    - Getting Started
    - School practice
    - Staff participation
    - Dealing with individual cases

Background to government policy on improving behaviour

The Home Office announced in 2004 that the government had undertaken the most radical reform of the Youth Justice System for 50 years. The reforms are focused on preventing offending amongst children and young people. The Crime and Disorder Act 1998 established the prevention of offending as the principle aim of the Youth Justice System and reform continued to progress under the Youth Justice and Criminal Evidence Act 1999.

National and local authority/police and school protocols

Review the national and local authority/police and school protocols, and any related policies and procedures.

As a headteacher you will need to ensure that the school policies and practice address the following areas:

- All schools are required to have a school behaviour, anti-bullying and discipline policy detailing the sanctions that will be imposed by the school when the school discipline policy is breached. This may include a list detailing the sanctions that will be implemented in cases of physical assault causing bodily harm requiring medical attention, sexual assault, robbery, criminal harassment and drug offences (for example, trafficking).
- Other occurrences which need to be addressed include incidents, threats of serious physical injury, incidents of vandalism, trespassing incidents and those that require referral to the local authority such as racial incidents. It may prove necessary to involve the police in these incidents after having appropriate discussions with parents.
- Agreed procedures with the local authority for information sharing and disclosure and the school reporting procedures.
- How school incidents are investigated, including those incidents involving pupils with special needs or where a pupil advocate may be required.
- Procedures for police interviews of pupils including:

  - notification of parents
  - preparation for interviews
  - conduct of interviews
  - pupil advocacy and support.

- School policy, for example, in the areas of search and confiscation, school detention.
- Procedures for referral where concerns exist or allegations are made regarding child protection issues.
- Occurrences involving children under the age of 16 and their rights to confidentiality.
- Non incident-related police involvement in the school.
- Prevention programmes such as violence prevention and crime prevention.
- Physical safety issues requiring a risk assessment being carried out by the school or local authority office.

Always refer to the local authority/school protocol.

 Search and confiscation

An overview

A search should be carried out in accordance with school policy. This policy should indicate if and when police should be contacted.

If you do proceed with a search, keep in mind the following:

- You must have reasonable grounds to believe that a breach of school discipline policy has occurred.
- The search is in line with the Violent Crime Reduction Act 2005 Power to Search.
- The search is implemented in line with school discipline policy.
- The search must be reasonable, not invasive.

When will a search be lawful?

1. When it is under the school discipline policy, or
2. When a personal search of a pupil is instigated using the powers under the Act to Search for an Offensive Weapon (Section 139 Criminal Justice Act 1988).

Who and why?

A headteacher or member of staff should carry out the search and/or confiscation where it is necessary in order to fulfil his or her duty to maintain proper order and discipline in the school.

A headteacher or member of staff must have reasonable grounds to believe there has been a breach of the school regulations or discipline policy and that a search of the pupil would reveal evidence of that breach.

Section 35 of the Violent Crime Reduction Act 2005 introduced new powers for schools to search school pupils if it is considered that there are reasonable grounds for believing that a pupil has a knife, a blade or an offensive weapon. The Act clarifies that a member of staff may search the pupil's outer clothing.

Legislation: The Education Act 1996, Section 550AA and Section 139 of the Criminal Justice Act 1998.

The young offender: implications for the school

Governance

Remember that police response will be in accordance with the local authority's police/school protocol. Outcomes will vary depending on the pupil's age.

The headteacher is responsible for maintaining order and discipline according to the adopted school behaviour and discipline policy. The police are responsible for enforcing where appropriate, the criminal code.

Record-keeping

Confidential information about young offenders may be disclosed to school representatives where necessary to ensure compliance of the young person with a court order, or to ensure the safety of staff, pupils or other persons. No person to whom this information is disclosed may disclose it to anyone else unless disclosure is necessary to ensure compliance or safety. The information must be kept separate from other records, be kept confidential and be destroyed when no longer needed for the reason it was disclosed.

School attendance

The DfES has been measuring progress on increased attendance with the aim to reduce the 2003 level of absence by 8% by 2008. This involves:

- new LA targets and data collections from schools
- data collection and analysis of the total absences each term and distinguished annually as authorized/unauthorized.

⊙ An overview

School attendance is an issue of pupil behaviour, but it is not necessarily a question of pupil discipline. The concern arises when parents refuse to send their child to school, or the pupil refuses to attend school. Chronic or habitual absence generally has a number of underlying causes. The best strategy is to deal immediately with any signs of tardiness, irregular attendance, poor academic performance or other signs of individual concern. In some communities there may be cultural patterns and historical factors at work as well.

Getting started

Headteachers should refer to national and local authority guidance before reviewing the school policy and procedures regarding pupil attendance. Review relevant legislation and local authority protocols for procedures and referrals. Schools should work closely with the Education Welfare Service to clarify respective responsibilities for enforcing school attendance, if pupils' poor attendance is a significant issue at the school.

School practice

Review the school's current prevention and intervention strategies for promoting, tracking, monitoring and reporting school attendance. Determine whether you are dealing with one or two individual instances of chronic absence, or a pattern of habitual absence of several pupils at the school. Plan your follow-up strategies accordingly; you may need to develop a more formal response if the latter is the case, through the Education Welfare Service.

Staff participation

Review with teachers any concerns or suggestions they have regarding pupil attendance. Discuss pupil assessment and evaluation practices in general, and the assessment and evaluation of frequently absent pupils in particular. Work with pastoral support teachers to review school attendance and develop strategies to engage pupils and involve others as appropriate.

Review all school policies, procedures and practices concerning attendance:

- first day report of absences to parents
- expectations regarding vacations, appointments and other out-of-school activities during regular school hours
- consequences for unexcused absences
- expectations of pupils regarding instruction and assignments they missed during an absence.

> To support schools, the DfES issued helpful advice in 2005, *Effective Attendance Practice in Schools – An Overview.*

Refer to DfES good practice and investigate what strategies are being used by schools facing similar circumstances. Discuss school attendance with relevant teachers and the Education Welfare Officer.

Where appropriate seek relevant agency support:

- the Education Welfare Service
- social workers
- psychologists
- local authority lead officer for child protection if there are child protection concerns.

Acquaint yourself with local authority policies and procedures regarding home tuition and other accommodations for long-term illness, home schooling and education otherwise than at school for pupils of compulsory school age.

The local authority Education Welfare Office (EWO) should make an assessment of the case and work with the family as well as the school to resolve issues surrounding poor school attendance. Protocols should be agreed between the EWO and the school to trigger a referral to the service.

Dealing with individual cases

Ensure that the pupil and parents clearly understand their obligations and responsibilities regarding compulsory school attendance. Enquire about any specific reasons for the habitual absence of an individual pupil. Provide support (including counselling) for individual pupils and parents through school staff and local authority staff (for example, a social worker).

Refer the pupil (with the consent of his or her parents) for assessment if necessary for special educational needs, or other relevant support through statutory or voluntary agencies, for example: Behaviour Support Services and the Child Adolescent and Mental Health Service.

Where pupils are identified as having a disability or having special educational needs, and possibly social, emotional or behavioural difficulties for a period of longer than 12 months, headteachers need to be mindful of their duties under the Disability Discrimination Acts 1995 and 2005 and the Special Educational Needs Disability Act 2001, to make reasonable adjustments in their discipline and attendance policies and, where necessary, justify the implementation of any sanctions imposed.

Special Educational Needs Disability Act 2001

This amended the Special Educational Needs framework, set out in the Education Act 1996 and extended the Disability Discrimination Acts 1995 to cover the provision of education. Since 2002, three duties have combined to provide a statutory framework that underpins equality of opportunity for disabled pupils in accessing school education:

- the disability discrimination duties in Part 4 of the Disability Discrimination Act
- the planning duties in Part 4 of the Disability Discrimination Act
- the special education needs duties in the Education Act 1996.

Relevant legislation

Education Act 1996

Duty on Parents – Section 7
Definition of Compulsory School Age
Prosecution of Parents (refer to the LA: Section 443 and Sections 444(1) and 444(1A))
Duty on Local Authorities Section 437

Children Act 1989

Education Supervision Order Local Authority
General Provisions for Welfare of Children

Pupil Education Registration Regulations issued in 1995, 1997 and 2006
Pupils' Attendance Records Regulations 1991
Education-related provision in the Anti-Social Behaviour Act 2003 covering:

- Section 19: parenting contracts
- Section 20: parenting orders
- Section 23: penalty notices

Schools will also need to be mindful of the legislation following the statutory inquiry into the death of Victoria Climbie (2003) and the joint Chief Inspectors' Report on Safeguarding Children (2002).

The government's response to these findings was included in the Green Paper, *Every Child Matters,* and the provisions in the Children Act 2004. These were followed by the Education and Inspection Act 2006 which introduces new powers for schools in the area of school behaviour and discipline covering pupil exclusions, with new guidance that followed in September 2006.

BE PREPARED

Be prepared. The day is never as you planned it.
Remember, the interruptions *are* the job.

PART 4
Health and Safety

24 Protecting our Pupils

Getting started

This chapter provides a very brief overview of a number of critical issues concerning at-risk children and young people. You will want to examine each of these topics in greater detail, within the context of your own school setting. Please note that the list of topics presented here is not exhaustive.

1. Follow your local authority policies, procedures and protocols governing the protection of pupils. Ensure that school procedures comply with local authority policies. Educate staff about their responsibilities and expected behaviours regarding protecting pupils.
2. Respect partnerships and protocols developed by the local authority for working with community agencies such as a child protection agency, probation officers, community resource centre, social services, the police, homeless shelters and women's shelters.

3. If there is a particular concern at the school (for example, bullying, significant child poverty), speak about the problem respectfully and honestly with all stakeholders. Keep protection of privacy in mind. Ensure privacy and protection for victims. Begin to seek support for the victims and the school community; access support from local authority personnel. Develop plans for long-term solutions.

Issues concerning at-risk children and youth

Access to information about pupils

Except for the right of the pupil (and the parent or guardian if a pupil is under the age of 18 years) to examine the pupil's record and to have a copy of the full record, such information is confidential. When the pupil reaches the age of 18 years, the parent or guardian has no right to information about the pupil without the pupil's permission.

If pupil information is required by the courts, consult local authority policy and the local authority legal department on how that information should be delivered.

Be mindful of your responsibility to control newspaper, radio and television access to pupils and to information about pupils. Follow local authority protocols regarding the publication of pupils' names and photos, the use of pupils' names on publicly displayed work, and other matters related to access to information about pupils. Seek parental permission for the release of names or any information about their children which might pose a risk to the child if the names or information got into the wrong hands.

Reporting suspected child abuse and neglect

TIP

> This is a critical aspect of your legal responsibilities; be sure that you understand thoroughly and follow carefully all local authority policies and procedures in this area.

What to report and when

If a person has reasonable grounds to suspect that a child has suffered harm or there is a risk that the child may suffer harm, the person must report the suspicion and the information on which it is based to the lead officer for child protection in the local authority, even when the information is discovered in a confidential manner. Further reports must be made if additional information is discovered. Read your local authority's protocol for child abuse thoroughly. Highlight the section with the procedures and have it on hand at all times.

Alleged misconduct or harassment by employees or volunteers toward a pupil

'Schools are intended to be healthy and nurturing environments within which children can safely grow and learn.

When a school environment is poisoned by sexual crimes or harassment, it is of fundamental concern to us all.'

(Robins, 2000, p. 1)

In the case of alleged misconduct or harassment by employees or volunteers towards a student, follow your local authority's policies and procedures. These may include procedures with titles such as 'Alleged employee misconduct towards a pupil' or 'Alleged harassment'.

Follow all local authority policies and procedures related to harassment, human rights, and so on.

TIP

When dealing with a situation of alleged misconduct or harassment, consult your local authority lead officer for child protection. Do not investigate the allegations until permission has been given by the local authority lead officer, in case police or social services wish to investigate first.

Using reasonable force for disciplinary purposes

Corporal punishment, hitting, physical punishment and chastisement of pupils is illegal.

Staff should be trained in legal restraint techniques to be used with minimum force if no other strategies are appropriate. This situation will only be appropriate in limited circumstances:

- self-defence
- prevention of significant damage to oneself, the miscreant or others
- when not to do so would be likely to lead to significant harm to others.

Though the law does allow minimum use of reasonable force to ensure good order and prevent major indiscipline, the dividing line between good order and an excessive use of force to make a child behave is a blurred line. There will always be the possibility of a dispute and a court case if school staff appear to exceed the minimum in their use of reasonable force to secure good behaviour. There is usually the option to walk away, and then impose a heavy sanction later on, if the pupil refuses to obey.

A good example would be a pupil refusing to stay in a detention. Rather than barring the exit and having an unseemly fracas at the doorway, staff would be better advised to let the pupil go, and then impose an exclusion the next day, for defiant refusal.

Action must be reasonable in the circumstances, taking into account the child's age, physical stature and level of maturity, the nature of the misbehavior, the method and severity of the punishment, and any resulting injury to the child.

Follow your local authority's policies and procedures governing the use of restraints with pupils. In some cases schools require parents whose children have been identified as having behavioral issues to sign an agreement permitting school staff to use restraints with the child, in accordance with agreed policy. Ensure proper training for staff who are likely to be required to restrain pupils in the course of their duties.

Document any use of force against pupils, for example, physically restraining a pupil from hitting another pupil by grabbing the child's arm (to stop the blow and preserve the safety of the other student).

Uses of force that go beyond what is 'reasonable' or that become the subject of a complaint by a parent or guardian must be reported to the local authority lead officer for child protection.

Missing and abducted children

Prevention strategies

1. Ensure that reliable adults always supervise the playground, school site and any field trips. Insist that school visitors and volunteers be identified with badges. Visitors must sign in. Follow the national requirements for criminal background checks for staff and volunteers.

2. Instruct pupils to report to an adult supervisor or go to the office if a stranger approaches them on the school grounds or in the school. Provide 'street proofing' instruction to children and teenagers on a regular basis.

3. Invite parents and guardians to call the school office in advance of a pupil absence. Call parents or guardians as soon as it is discovered that a pupil is missing from school without prior notification, and there is any reason to believe that something untoward might have happened.

   Do not permit younger pupils to leave school with an adult other than the pupil's parent or a prearranged, responsible person. Ensure that all parents and guardians sign pupils out when leaving the school and sign pupils in when arriving at school during the working day. All pupils must sign in and out, if unaccompanied, if they leave during the working day.

4. Consider alerting the police regarding strangers near the school or the grounds, or regarding vehicles that are parked next to the school for no apparent reason. Record the make, model, and licence plate number of the vehicle.

5. Do not post pictures of children except in compliance with local authority policy. See Chapter 5, 'Communication', and Chapter 9, 'Records and Information Management', for further information regarding publication, protection of privacy and pupil safety. Link the school's website to other sites which offer information to parents and guardians about prevention and protection strategies for children.

If a pupil is missing

- Check the school. Call parents/guardians.
- The first 24 hours are critical to the safe return of the child.
- Call the police: describe the student's clothing, location last seen and possible route taken.
- Obtain names of witnesses.
- Inform your local authority.

The rights of non-custodial parents

Alerts

Alert office staff and teachers if there are concerns that an adult without access rights or of an unsuitable nature will attempt to see the child or obtain information about the child. File court orders and other pertinent family data in the pupil record files.

Ask for written identification from any persons not well known to the school when they request information about a pupil or wish to remove a pupil from the school. Train all staff, regular and occasional, not to give out any information about any pupil without authorization.

If you suspect the child is in immediate danger, or if the adult or parent is being disruptive, call the police.

Custody

Unless the court orders otherwise, a spouse who is granted access to a child of the marriage has the right to make enquiries, and to be given information, as to the health, education and welfare of the child.

Access

Access rights of a parent, regardless of whether or not the child lives with that parent, may be varied or denied only by written separation agreement or court order. When a non-custodial parent requests physical access to a child, provide the access based on the provisions in the separation agreement or court order.

The custodial parent is the primary contact person who makes day-to-day decisions; this is the individual with whom the school will have the most interaction for issues such as attendance, field trips, course selection, and so on.

Although it is the responsibility of the custodial parent to share educational information with the non-custodial parent, the non-custodial parent should receive from the school such information as reports, sports day information, invitations and newsletters according to local authority expectations.

Do not get involved in issues relating to family domestic situations. Do not take sides or imply that one parent is more worthy than the other. Do not follow instructions in any letter from any lawyer without first getting clearance from your, or the local authority, legal advisor.

Bullying

Schools need to establish a social climate where physical aggression and bullying are not used to gain popularity, maintain group leadership, or influence others to do what they are told to do.
No one deserves to be bullied.
More information on bullying is available in 'What schools can do' at www.bullybeware.com.

Collaboration

Listen to what pupils, teachers and parents and guardians have to say about the occurrence of bullying in the school. Find ways to involve the school governing body, the pupils and the community in developing a comprehensive schoolwide antibullying plan. Collaborate with staff (for example, social workers) to identify local authority-sponsored anti-bullying programmes. Consult headteachers in other schools; review programmes and strategies in place elsewhere.

Code of conduct

Review school policies and the school code of conduct. The school policy should include a clear definition of bullying and how the school will respond to incidents. The school code of conduct should state the school's commitment to the prevention of bullying.

Provide training for staff, and provide resources for integrating anti-bullying education into the educational programmes at all year levels.

Supervision

> 'Headteachers must make it clear that bullying is never acceptable.'
>
> (Ross, 1998, p. 44)

Recognize the covert nature of bullying and that most bullying happens during breaks or in unstructured time. Encourage pupils to report incidents of bullying and to understand the difference between telling tales, reporting and taking care of oneself and others. Provide increased supervision in areas where bullying tends to occur, and provide alternative play areas and quiet spaces for pupils who are fearful. Recognize and reward pupils and staff for positive acts of school citizenship.

See Chapter 3, 'Negligence and Liability', for further information regarding supervision of pupils and also Chapter 22, 'Pupil Behaviour and Discipline in the School'.

Response

Encourage communication, foster empathy for others and insist on accountability for personal behaviour. Refer frequently to the school's code of conduct. Consistently enforce school policy in the playground, classrooms and hallways, and in e-mail correspondence; apply consequences for bullies. Train staff in effective classroom management and supervision strategies, and support their implementation of the school's anti-bullying plan. Introduce programmes such as peer mediation, a buddy system, and social skills and anger management workshops; teach assertiveness and social skills.

When victims are identified, demonstrate concern, keep records, protect the pupil from further attacks, inform parents or guardians of both the bully and the victim, and administer consequences to the bully.

Call the police when a pupil or pupils are suspected of continued serious coercion and inflicting physical or emotional harm. Refer to your local authority's police/school protocol.

Implementation and monitoring
Launch the anti-bullying plan at an assembly; provide brochures or information on the school's website and in newsletters for parents and guardians. Keep a log of bullying incidents to recognize patterns. Address the concerns of a parent or guardian whose child is an alleged bully or victim. Take steps to identify best practices in other schools.

Looked after children with disadvantaged home backgrounds

Barriers to education
Pupils with domestic/residential difficulties may be behind in school because of transience and absenteeism. Secondary school pupils may experience great difficulty in completing exam courses. Pupils may not make friends, participate in class discussions or relate easily with teachers. Such pupils may come to school less than well fed and be unable to pay for school meals, school supplies, after-school activities, tickets for social events, transportation, and so on.

These children often have little or no involvement with stimulating activities to promote their physical and intellectual growth. Pupils living in temporary accommodation may not develop study skills or have a place to study. Some pupils may not have developed age-appropriate life skills and may lack essential health and dental care. During vacation periods, young children may be left alone in unsafe situations.

Health records, transcripts, birth certificates, guardianship records, special education information and the pupil's records may be hard to track down.

Strategies

1. Foster a school climate that will nurture disadvantaged pupils and provide for stability, security, belonging, friendship and adult support. Educate the staff and governing body about homelessness and poverty. Seek creative ways to offer before- and after-school programmes, weekend, holiday and summer programmes, and tutoring for transient children. Ensure that children and young people have access to school supplies, a place to store personal belongings, clothes, hygiene products, nutritious meals, a place to study, recreational activities and sports equipment, and transportation. Look to the extended school agenda to provide greater community involvement for disadvantaged pupils.
2. Follow local authority procedures for enrolling pupils without permanent addresses and follow protocols for sharing information about transient pupils and their families. Enquire about tracking of transient pupils. If a pupil must move out of the school's immediate area, attempt to find transportation so the pupil can continue in the same school, in accordance with local authority policies. Report to the child protection agency children under the age of 18 who have no apparent parent or guardian or fixed address, or who are runaways.
3. Develop partnerships with local community social agencies and shelters. Provide information to pupils and parents or guardians regarding community resources and health services. Although it is necessary to protect personal privacy, share information with community social agencies about the needs of homeless children and young people. Through shelters and community support programmes, share information about school programmes with parents or guardians and carers of homeless children and young people.

Many of the above barriers and strategies concerning homeless children and young people are also relevant to children living in poverty or in shelters.

TIP

LOOK AFTER YOURSELF

You will spend a lot of time looking after others. Be sure to look after yourself too.
Determine your priorities in life: personal health, family, friends and work.
Learn how to manage stress: read the literature, take a workshop, develop an action plan to deal with stress.
If you have children of your own, give them permission to have a balanced life by modelling that yourself.

25 Occupational Health and Safety

At a glance

- Getting started
- Duties of the headteacher
- Conducting a school safety inspection
- Developing occupational health and safety procedures

→ Getting started

Consider how you would handle the following issues:

- A hazardous chemical is seeping into the school's water system.
- The floor in the gymnasium is chipped and cracked.
- Staff who use the temporary huts are complaining of headaches and increased asthma attacks.
- The temperature within the building is above 80°F during warm May and June days.
- The entrances to the school during winter are not cleared of snow and are frequently slippery.

Duties of the headteacher

1. Health and Safety legislation stipulates the responsibilities of the employer (local authority in community schools and the governing body in foundation, voluntary aided and independent schools) and the role of headteachers in administrating and enforcing the legislation. The employer is responsible for ensuring health and safety, so far as is

reasonably practicable, through its policies and procedures including risk assessments.

(a) Examine the employer's occupational health and safety policy and procedures.
(b) Review related employer policies and procedures; these may cover topics ranging from smoking on school premises to information systems designed to reduce the risk from hazardous products in the workplace.
(c) Review collective agreements for clauses related to occupational health and safety.

2. Some of the duties of senior management may include ensuring, so far as you reasonably can, that workers:

(a) work in the manner and with the protective measures and procedures that the workers' employer requires
(b) use or wear the equipment, protective devices or clothing that the workers' employer requires to be used or worn
(c) know of the existence of any potential or actual danger to their health or safety.

3. In addition, you have many other related duties, including:

(a) maintaining proper order and discipline in the school
(b) giving careful attention to the health and comfort of the pupils; to the cleanliness, temperature, and ventilation of the school; to the care of all teaching materials and other school property; to the condition and appearance of the school property; and to the condition and appearance of the school buildings and grounds
(c) reporting promptly to the employer when you have reason to suspect the existence of any communicable disease in the school or of any unsanitary condition on any part of the school buildings or grounds
(d) inspecting the school premises regularly and reporting forthwith to the employer if repairs to the school are, in your opinion, required
(e) reporting to the employer any lack of effectiveness on the part of the building maintenance staff
(f) arranging for regular emergency fire drills. (*Note:* these emergency drills must be held during times in which lessons are being given, including evening classes or classes conducted outside the school year.)

You have these duties and responsibilities because you have the management authority and control over the situations described. With delegated power comes the delegated responsibility to use the powers in a healthy and safe manner.

Conducting a school safety inspection

'The goal of a workplace inspection should be to identify hazards that can lead to injury/illness or property damage.'

(Avery, 2002, p. 3)

1. Consult your employer's policy about the frequency and types of inspections required. Ensure the appropriate involvement of unions when scheduling and carrying out inspections. Involve the school staff in assisting with inspections and use this as a strategy to raise awareness about safety issues and continuous improvement.
2. Establish procedures and terms of reference for the school safety inspections. Facilitate training on recognition and identification of hazards.

   ✓ Prepare a school walk-through checklist to gather specific information in areas such as:

   - hall
   - classrooms
   - common areas, including the cafeteria, car park, hallways and entrances
   - private study rooms
   - library and computer laboratories
   - photography darkrooms
   - physical education facilities, including swimming pools
   - playing fields and playgrounds
   - portable classrooms
   - science laboratories
   - technology workshops
   - arts rooms.

Before the inspection, review past reports to identify problem areas.

What to look for in a standard classroom inspection

Fire safety

- Are legible fire exit and route signs in appropriate locations?
- Is there a Fire Safety Plan and is the teacher aware of the content and location of the plan?
- Are ceilings or exit doors free of combustible material such as artwork, posters, paper, and so on? As a guideline, no more than 20 per cent of the total wall surface (including boards, windows, and so on) is to be covered with combustible materials.
- Where there is an exit door, is there a clear path around the classroom furniture? As a rule of thumb, the width of the clear path should be the same as the width of the door(s).

Electrical

- Are electrical safety approval labels on all electrical equipment?
- Are electrical outlets, cover plates and wall switches secure and undamaged?
- Are extension cords three-wire, in good condition, and used for temporary purposes only?
- Are multiuse cords equipped with power bars?

General

- Do windows open easily and stay open according to their design?
- Do air quality, temperature and ventilation meet applicable standards? Concerns may be determined by conversation with the teacher in the classroom.
- Are ventilation and heating ducts kept unobstructed by books, paper, and so on?
- Are ceiling tiles in place and unbroken, with no sign of mould formation?
- Are the ceiling, walls and floor free from water leaks?
- Are floor tiles or carpeting securely fastened to reduce trip hazards?
- Are floors free from hazards that could cause slips, trips and falls?
- Are audiovisual screens and maps securely suspended using fittings designed for the purpose?

- Are shelves or shelving units firmly anchored to the wall? Storage of all items should follow the following guide: heavy objects on low shelves, light objects on high shelves and breakable objects such as glass items on low shelves.
- Are step stools or small ladders available for accessing stored items from high shelves?
- Is storage on top of wall-mounted cupboards limited to lightweight objects such as empty boxes?
- Do paper-cutters have guards in place and is the torsion spring adjusted to hold the blade up when released?
- Are there first aid stations and trained first aiders available? Do all staff know where the stations are located, and are the trained staff locations identified?
- Is there an asbestos management programme and do all staff know where an asbestos log is kept in school?

3. After the inspection, consult with employer health and safety personnel and community health agencies for information, advice, and solutions to problems. Report recommendations to the employer. Recommendations could include ways to eliminate hazards, upgrade facilities and equipment to meet legislative standards, improve hygiene practices, and meet ongoing maintenance requirements.

Develop plans for foreseeable contingencies

Be sure to have a plan in place to deal with health and safety situations which may arise. For example, know what you will do if the science, physical education, technology or music teacher (or any other teacher in a higher risk area) is absent.

Developing occupational health and safety procedures

1. Consult your employer's policies and procedures for direction on how to deal with particular areas of the school. If you do not find the elements listed below in your employer's procedures, do consider them when developing your school's health and safety procedures, and seek your employer's advice on what should be included:

(a) asbestos
(b) art supplies
(c) athletic equipment and facilities
(d) blackboards and white boards
(e) ergonomics
(f) fire safety
(g) first aid kits, eye wash stations and non-latex gloves
(h) floors, entrances and walkways
(i) food safety and cafeteria services
(j) mould and mildew
(k) new carpeting, painting or construction
(l) pesticides, toxic materials and other hazardous materials
(m) printing and duplicating equipment
(n) routine maintenance and cleanliness
(o) staff training
(p) vehicle safety
(q) ventilation, lighting, heating, electrical and cooling systems
(r) washrooms and drinking water.

2. Ensure the staff know who the members of the safety committee are and
know how to report concerns or questions. Be constantly vigilant that
staff comply with health and safety legislation, employer policy and
school procedures. Post signs and health and safety information in the
staffroom, common areas of the school and classrooms, as appropriate.
Include occupational health and safety issues on the agendas of staff,
department head and governing body meetings, and in school newsletters
and on the website.

For further information, see Chapter 3, 'Negligence and Liability'.

TIP

26 Emergency Preparedness

Getting started

'... it is now the headteacher's responsibility to plan for the unexpected, prepare for the unthinkable, and ensure that everything that can be done, is done, in case of an emergency'.

(Stevens, 2001, p. 54)

Review your local authority's policy and procedures regarding school safety and emergency preparedness. These may include procedures for fire alarms, bomb threats, violent incidents, armed intruders and severe weather. Because each school building, location, community and pupil body is different, headteachers need to assess their school's ability to respond to a variety of emergencies; for example, response plans will be different in rural and urban areas.

Review the school's crisis response plan and team. Meet with the team for a briefing.

Study the school crisis response plan. Some questions for your consideration are noted in the two sections below.

1.   Staff and pupil preparedness

Will the staff know what to do if the headteacher is not in the building?

Is there a written emergency plan that includes a fire plan and a communication plan?

Is there a folder or other type of organized information system to provide critical information during an emergency?

Do both regular and occasional staff understand the plan and have assigned duties and training?

Are code words for emergencies such as bomb threats or lockdown situations clearly understood by all staff?

Is there an emergency/crisis response team with each member having clearly defined responsibilities?

Are drills for various emergencies conducted and evaluated regularly?

What is the procedure for reporting staff or pupil accidents or injuries?

Are safety procedures and behavioural expectations described in the pupil handbook and are consequences stipulated in the code of conduct?

Is the governing body aware of the school's crisis response planning and preparation?

2.   Safety equipment

Is equipment (for example, torches and walkie-talkies) readily available?

Are first aid kits maintained, distributed throughout the building, and available for field trips?

What type of communication systems are there between classrooms, other areas of the school and the main office? Does the public announcement system have emergency power backup?

Do the headteacher, deputy headteacher and staff supervisor(s) carry walkie-talkies, beepers or mobile phones when supervising the building or grounds?

How are exterior doors positioned in relation to the school grounds and surrounding community? Are they locked during school hours?

Is there an off-site evacuation location for pupils and staff? Does the school serve as an evacuation centre for another school or community agency?
Are there regular inspections of the building and school grounds to ensure proper maintenance, functionality of mechanical systems, and appropriate storage and disposal of hazardous materials?

Preventative measures

Emergency Response Committee

Use the local authority model to develop the school response protocol. Include school staff, local authority security personnel, union representatives, members of the governing body and community resource persons in the review of the existing school response procedures. Identify problem areas and recommend response protocols.

Assign specific roles to each member of the Emergency Response Committee; for example, crowd control, equipment coordinator, internal communications, trauma and grief counselling, first aid and parent support.

Conduct an annual evaluation of the crisis response plan. Update equipment and review staff functions.

Emergency response plan

1. Issues
Location of the school in relation to potential community hazards.
Distance from community medical and emergency help.
Size and design of the school building and location of entrances and exits.
Availability of off-site evacuation facilities.
Age and size of the pupil body.
Availability of district services.

2. Types of emergencies
Accident or fire in the community.
Assault or suspected rape.
Bomb threat.
Building system or mechanical malfunction.
Chemical or other hazardous spill.
Death of a pupil or staff member at school or at home.
Drug overdose, poisoning or allergic reaction.

Field trip incident.
Fire in the school.
Intruder or confrontational person.
Kidnapping, hostage situation, missing child, or murder.
Large group disturbance or gang fight.
Severe weather or earthquake.
Shooting or use of other weapon.

> Evaluate each crisis individually to determine the appropriate level of response.   **TIP**

3.   The fire plan

Ensure that the school has an up-to-date fire plan and keep copies in the main office, head's office, staff room and other appropriate areas of the school.

Annually inspect each room or area of the school to make certain that the fire exits and exit routes are clearly marked.

Inspect exit routes and doors frequently to ensure they are unobstructed.

4.   Crisis communication

Follow district policies and procedures on crisis communication.
Review school level communication protocols with staff.
Design a simple communication strategy:

- Identify who needs to be notified.
- Specify plans for getting information out.
- Identify responsibility centres.

Prepare a format for messages delivered by staff via phone and the public announcement system. File samples of the following:

- letters of condolence
- information letters to parents
- news releases.

File the district media or public relations kit.
Establish contacts with emergency personnel in the community.
Foster a positive relationship with the local media.

Equipment and information

1. Equipment

Stock emergency kits for the main office and other key areas of the school as required. Kits should include the following:

- class lists
- mobile phones
- pagers or walkie-talkies
- emergency phone numbers
- torches
- radio with batteries
- battery operated loudhailer
- blankets
- office supplies.

Ensure ready access to first aid supplies including non-latex gloves.
Prepare a folder that contains the following:

- a copy of the response plan and other important information
- a list of first aid qualified staff
- a list of pupils with special medical or mobility needs
- phone numbers for bus companies, municipal emergency services and local authority security personnel
- maps of the school indicating special areas, utilities shut-off sites, and hazardous materials
- the official fire plan.

Place copies of the binder in the main office, caretaker/site manager's office and other key areas of the building.

2. Communication

Establish signals for lockdowns, pupil and staff medical emergencies, bomb threats and an all-clear to return to the building.

Have a map of the off-site evacuation location and procedures for transporting pupils there and registering attendance upon arrival.

Establish protocols with the other schools or community agencies for which your school serves as an evacuation site.

Evacuations and other emergency responses

Assign staff to serve as area wardens to assist with the supervision of evacuations, to communicate instructions when there is no public address system and to give the all-clear signal once the building has been cleared.

Conduct fire and emergency drills as required by employer policy. Evaluate the results.

Train staff in evacuation procedures; for example, taking the most recent attendance record with them in an evacuation or locking the door when the area is cleared in a lockdown.

Train staff and secondary school pupils not to go to the car park or remove their vehicles in emergencies.

Develop evacuation procedures that include staging areas for pupils to assemble when they leave the building, the involvement of fire, police, ambulance or emergency measures personnel, and provision for disabled or special needs pupils.

Consider when to use lockdowns to keep pupils behind locked classroom doors and what to do with pupils who may be in common areas.

Consult the local authority's procedures regarding conditions under which you can send home pupils and staff in an emergency.

Reactive strategies

Take control

Assess the situation and determine the level and type of response. For example, a hazardous spill may require an immediate evacuation; an armed intruder may require a lockdown; a boiler failure may require calling the buses to take pupils home.

Activate the portion of the emergency response plan or fire plan appropriate to the situation. Provide immediate first aid. Ensure a safe evacuation staging area and protection from inclement weather. Investigate and search as required.

In the event of a bomb threat, do not touch anything and do not use shortwave radios or mobile phones that might activate the bomb.

Call for emergency assistance

When you call for assistance, give specific information to the police, ambulance and firefighters. Do not move any victims; call immediately for help. Cooperate with fire, police and medical personnel when they arrive.

Inform parents and guardians of pupil victims and ensure they have transportation to the hospital. When no parent is available to be with a pupil at the hospital, send a staff member.

Give specific information when calling for emergency assistance

'There are approximately 45 students and others at the front of the school building. Some have knives and baseball bats and they are threatening to assault each other.'

'The pupil is an 11-year-old girl who has recently been diagnosed as a diabetic. She is currently unconscious and her pulse is weak and thready. Her father has been called. He is five minutes way from the school. What is your estimated time of arrival?'

Communicate, communicate, communicate

1. Keep notes about calls, responses and procedures. Document, document, document.
2. Get assistance from the local authority's communications officer. Draft verbal and printed statements or news releases that give a brief outline of the incident and indicate how updates can be obtained.
3. Do not release names of pupils and staff involved in the incident until parents and family have been notified.
4. Share information with parents, pupils, the governing body, the local authority, neighbouring schools, community agencies that are housed in the school building, and so on, as directed by the local authority's communications officer.
5. Get all the bad news out at once; then talk only about the actions the school is taking.
6. Provide interviews with the media relaying your three key messages. You may wish to provide interviews through the local authority's communications officer. If you do not have a local authority communications officer to assist you with preparations for interviews or press conferences, call the press and media expert at your professional association.
7. Do not place blame; state the facts and talk about the solution.
8. Understand what the headteacher is responsible for; do not speak on behalf of the police, health unit or anyone else.

If the incident occurs at the weekend or during a holiday, it may be necessary to open the school for use by staff, parents and pupils.

See Chapter 6, 'Public and Media Relations', for further information on dealing with the media and conducting interviews.

Follow-up and evaluation

1. All-clear

Ensure the building is safe for the return of staff and pupils after an evacuation. Provide for alternative teaching space if a portion of the building is under repair after fire, vandalism, flooding, and so on. If the school has been seriously damaged or destroyed, seek assistance from your local authority staff and community organizations to find temporary space and learning materials.

2. Debriefing

Assemble the school's emergency response team and review their actions. Seek their advice and suggestions. Meet with all staff and brief them. Seek the assistance of the local authority's tragic events team and staff from other schools.

3. Communication

Prepare a statement for staff members to use when answering phone inquires. Meet with pupils in small groups to provide follow-up information and answer questions. In some instances, an assembly may be appropriate. Follow local authority procedures for the reporting of pupil accidents and staff accidents. With the guidance of the local authority information officer, prepare a letter for parents, the local community, the media, and so on, to offer additional information about the incident and what pupils can expect.

4. In case of death

Generally, the local authority will have developed a process for all schools. Call the family of the victim(s); indicate your concern and offer the support services of the local authority. Open a book of condolence in the main office or other suitable location. Determine whether the school will hold a memorial service for the deceased and help pupils and staff with the planning. Close pupil or staff records according to local authority procedures. Deal with the victim's personal effects.

Provide rooms where pupils can meet with peer and staff counsellors. Consult with the emergency/crisis response team about how staff and pupils are coping during the aftermath; identify issues and concerns. Pupil suicide will require special steps to minimize the possibility that other pupils may imitate the behaviour. Seek guidance from relevant personnel.

Arrange for class coverage for staff who wish to attend the funeral.

Training opportunities

Take advantage of all training offered by your local authority in the area of emergency preparedness.

CONTROL YOUR REACTIONS AND TAKE RESPONSIBILITY

Always remember that your response sets the tone for everyone else's.
You may not be able to control circumstances, but you can control the way you react to them.
When you make a mistake (and that will happen), take full responsibility and apologize.

27 Pupil Medical Needs

⮕ Getting started

Governing body and/or local authority policies and procedures and school practices

Follow these policies and procedures regarding pupil health issues. The policies might include the following topics:

- administration of medication to pupils and providing for their health needs
- anaphylaxis
- communicable diseases
- first aid and training

- HIV/AIDS/hepatitis
- reporting an accident or injury.

> The employer (local authority or governing body) is responsible for ensuring so far as is reasonably practicable the health (and safety) needs of pupils.

With the advent of inclusion it is to be expected that numbers of pupils who have some major health issue or needs will be welcomed into mainstream schools.

There is no legal or contractual requirement on school staff to administer medicines or to provide for a pupil's health needs. It is unwise to volunteer to do so as it extends your personal duty of care, may set a precedent, may not be insured and is not the purpose for which you, as a member of the school staff, were appointed.

The ideal solution is for the employer to arrange for a member of staff to be *under contract*, suitably trained and freely accepting the contractual responsibility for providing health care; this person would be a quasi-school nurse and would need an appropriate rate of pay. This scenario is the opposite of volunteering.

First aid
The employer is responsible for arranging for sufficient and suitable first aiders to provide first aid cover. First aid is for unexpected emergency health situations and does not cover regular, known or likely health issues.

Anaphylaxis – use of 'epi-pens'
Use of 'epi-pens' to administer an emergency dose of adrenalin in the event of collapse due to anaphylactic shock or extreme allergic response is, technically, a health provision and does not feature in first aid training.

However if it is known that a pupil is likely to suffer a reaction, and an 'epi-pen' is available, it might be difficult to justify to a court or to a grieving parent why an attempt was not made to save life by administering the 'epi-pen' as best as one can, while waiting for the ambulance.

This is an exclusive and singular concession – in general, staff cannot be expected to go beyond first aid training unless they are qualified school nurses.

Administration of medication – general principles
Sometimes pupils can self-medicate if they are old enough or responsible enough. At other times parents, friends or neighbours can, with parental permission, come into school and administer medical treatment. All the school needs to do is to make such meetings possible and private. Of course, pupils can go home for treatment and then return.

The reserve position for the school is that if a child appears unwell or in need of medical care, then parents may be invited to take the child home or, in an emergency, an ambulance would be summoned via the usual 999 telephone route.

Communicable and infectious diseases
If it seems likely that communicable or infectious disease might be prevalent among the school community then advice needs to be urgently sought from the local health services communicable disease experts.

HIV/AIDS/hepatitis
Schools may become aware that pupils or staff are suffering potentially lethal conditions. As schools are not allowed to disclose confidential medical information to the wider community, it will be necessary to *assume* that, in any incident of accident or illness, it is *possible* that individuals involved might be infected or carriers, whether they know about it or not.

When bodily fluids – blood, saliva and so on – are involved in the incident it is essential that careful sanitation and cleansing approaches are used: face masks, protective gloves, disinfectants, and so on. The school should have a clear policy about dealing with bodily fluids.

Reporting an accident or injury
The employer and local authority may wish to know the details of any injury. They will advise you of any health and safety legislation requirements such as the Reporting of Injuries, Diseases and Dangerous Occurrences (RIDDOR) scheme which needs a report.

It is reasonable for the school to ask what use will be made of the accident or injury reports; reports should generate improved strategies to reduce the future likelihood of accidents or injuries.

Prevention programmes

Communicate regularly to all parents and pupils the steps being taken at the school to reduce health risks for pupils. Ensure that individual pupils with health issues are not identified. Be prepared to address the attitudes and concerns that some staff, pupils and parents may have regarding any new prevention protocols being implemented at the school.

Involve the staff and governing body in the planning of prevention and intervention programmes. Determine what outside resources are available to assist with prevention programming. Develop prevention programmes in partnership with community agencies and the health department. Implement appropriate prevention programmes (for example, peanut-free programmes designed to reduce health risks). Evaluate the school's prevention programmes regularly.

Reduce the risk for pupils with life-threatening allergies and chronic conditions through careful planning that takes into account such factors as cafeteria services and menus, accommodation for eating lunch, risks on field trips, school painting and maintenance protocols, and the use of non-toxic cleaning materials and pesticides.

Administration of medication to pupils

1. As has been said earlier, it is ideal if there is a member of staff available and under contract to provide health care.
2. When reviewing your employer's arrangements for administering medication and providing health care, consider the elements noted in the areas below.

    (a) The availability of qualified staff, the provision of staff training, and the creation of an updated list of designated staff;
    the degree to which administering medication interferes with other regular duties of staff.
    (b) Any authorization form to be signed by the parent;
    the possible side effects involved in administering the medication.
    (c) The number of pupils requiring medication regularly or on an as-needed basis; the various types of medication provided and their storage requirements (for example, refrigeration);
    labelling of all medications and photographic identification of pupil.
    (d) Medication storage:

    a protocol for checking the age of medication;
    a location for safe, secure, and accessible storage of medications.

(e) Medication administration:

a private location for administering or supervising the administration of medication;

the use of log sheets to record details regarding the administration of medication, including pupil's name, date, time of administration, dosage given and name of person administering;

a response plan for dealing with emergencies arising from the administering of medication;

procedures for administering medication or emergency treatment when pupils are off-site.

All of the above issues regarding the management of the medical provision are for the employer to arrange and the headteacher to cooperate with, and does *not* include the headteacher providing any personal medical care.

Other health issues

Chronic illness

Within the context of local authority policy, develop proactive and reactive school procedures and classroom strategies to help staff and pupils understand chronic illnesses and conditions such as asthma, diabetes, epilepsy, cancer, cystic fibrosis, juvenile rheumatoid arthritis, haemophilia, mental illness, HIV/AIDS and muscular dystrophy. Staff may have an understanding of the medical condition and skills in emergency management that are specific to the individual pupil.

Acquaint yourself with local authority policies and procedures regarding home tuition and other accommodations for long-term illness. Find out what supports are available through local authority staff (for example, social workers and psychologists) and outside agencies to assist chronically ill pupils and their parents.

Ensure that pupils with restricted mobility are considered in the development of evacuation plans and fire safety training.

A comprehensive school health programme

'While we expect our schools to be places of learning, the role we expect them to play in health is not clearly defined.

> If our schools could promote health as they do learning, holistically and with measures available, the benefits both today and to future generations would be very significant – both in terms of heath and education.'
> (*A National Framework for Health Promoting Schools 2000–2003*)

When developing a comprehensive school health plan, follow your local authority policies and procedures, the curriculum guidelines and various special education requirements. As you develop your plan, consider (among others) the factors listed below.

Social, medical and physical support

Counselling, psychological, and social services provided by the local authority and others.
Referrals to, and partnerships with, community agencies.
Trauma and grief counselling.
Peer counsellors, peer helpers and peer support groups.
Mentoring.
Teacher adviser programmes.
Stress management programmes for staff and pupils.
Staff wellness programmes.
Health screening and fitness testing and promotion.
Healthy role models.
Modifications to the school building and classrooms for wheelchairs and other aspects of disabled access.

Preventative health

1. Review the preventative health programmes currently offered through the curriculum, which might include the following:

   (a) safe driving and impaired driving
   (b) smoking cessation
   (c) substance abuse
   (d) suicide
   (e) eating disorders
   (f) head lice
   (g) sun protection and skin cancer

(h) sexually transmitted diseases and hepatitis
(i) sexual abstinence
(j) date rape.

Several of the above intervention programmes are culturally sensitive and require careful handling.

2. Review the services currently offered at the school or through the local authority for school-age pupils that contribute to a comprehensive school health programme:

(a) services related to speech, hearing and sight
(b) dental and oral health services
(c) nutrition, weight management and cafeteria services
(d) mental health and depression services
(e) school-based health centres (treatment and rehabilitation)
(f) after-school programmes
(g) preschool and school readiness programmes
(h) school and community social workers and psychologists
(i) health unit
(j) physicians
(k) police
(l) fire department.

Further reading regarding pupil health

Anderson, A. (ed.) (2001) Healthy schools/healthy kids, special issue of Orbit.
Greene, L.E. (ed.) (2002) Children's health & safety, special issue of Principal.

CALL ON COLLEAGUES: BUILD A NETWORK

Talk with colleagues. They are a source and a resource.
Just knowing that there is someone out there who can help is a great comfort.
Gather wisdom from those who have more experience than you do.

28 School Off-site Activities and Field Trips

An overview

School off-site activities take place during the regular school day as part of the educational programme (for example, a visit to a museum), and sometimes outside of school hours as part of the taught curriculum.

Traditionally, pupil activities have also included activities which are not strictly curriculum based but form an important part of a pupil's wider education, such as:

- science fairs, public speaking and debating
- pupil council and other pupil volunteer activities in the school

- school newspapers and yearbooks
- interschool sports, athletics and swimming
- arts performances (music, drama, dance)
- community service groups and other special interest clubs
- after-school programmes and homework clubs
- school celebration days and entertainment activities
- adventurous activities in 'wild' country.

These activities might be described as 'leisure and recreational' as they have no direct National Curriculum link, but are nevertheless an important part of the education process to:

- motivate pupils
- develop leadership and other social skills
- promote positive self-concepts
- provide a vehicle to create inclusion
- link academic learning with practical skills
- stimulate school ethos
- foster regular attendance
- recognize pupils for nonacademic talents.

Source: adapted from Thompson, 1993, pp.10–6 and 10–7.

School activities and field trips: getting started

Review the local authority's policy and procedures regarding leisure and recreational activities and field trips. Scrutinize the school's policies and procedures concerning leisure and recreational activities and field trips to ensure they are in compliance with the local authority policies. When planning a school activity or field trip involving physical activities, review safety guidelines and safety requirements. Review the previous year's school plan regarding these activities and field trips. Seek advice/approval from the local authority off-site education officer.

Recognize staff, pupils, parents and community members who contribute to the school's activities and field trip programme. Respect the workload and family responsibilities of staff, pupils and parents when planning the off-site activities programme.

Identify barriers and challenges; for example, access to bus services after school hours, programme costs, safety concerns, workload for a small staff, lack of facilities, and attitudes (for example, beliefs that the leisure and recreational programme robs time from the educational curriculum).

Design creative partnerships among parents, staff, volunteers and community organizations to help overcome some of the barriers that you may encounter.

> **Supervision of school activities**
>
> The headteacher of a school must provide for the supervision of and the conducting of any school activity authorised by the local authority or governing body. The head-teacher is responsible for off-site as well as on-site activities although he/she does not have to be physically present, merely confident that reasonable arrangements have been made to ensure safety and provide high quality education.

Planning and organization

In planning a field trip or leisure and recreational programme, consider the following factors:

- relevant local authority policies and procedures
- authorization of the particular activity, by local authority, governing body, headteacher
- supervision – staffing ratios, teachers, staff, volunteers
- potential risks, safety and health issues
- the educational value of the activity
- preventing and reporting injuries
- transportation
- budgeting, costs and fund-raising
- coverage for staff who are out of the classroom or school
- cultural equity and inclusion
- recruitment and training of volunteers
- community partners
- permission forms and record-keeping
- special needs of participating pupils (consider pupils' gender, language, culture, race, ethnicity, religion, sexual orientation, disabilities, and so on)
- communication and consultation with staff, parents, pupils and the school governing body
- voluntary nature of leisure and recreational activities.

Fund-raising

The educational curriculum both on and off site is free to pupils and is funded by the delegated budget. Leisure and recreational activities are voluntary and should not be subsidized from the delegated budget, but fully costed by subscription from the participants. Voluntary donations towards educational activities can be made at any time. No child can be precluded from an educational visit (that is, directly related to the curriculum) because there has been no financial contribution from the family. Any activity can, of course, be the target for general fund-raising.

Use appropriate accounting and auditing practices for all fund-raising; for example:

- submit all money raised for educational activities to the delegated school account and to a separate identifiable account for leisure and recreational events
- issue receipts where appropriate or as directed by local authority policy
- follow local authority procedures for governing body and parent fundraising initiatives.

For further information, see the section in Chapter 10, 'Budget and Resource Management' dealing with funds not part of the delegated budget.

Assemblies and special events (daytime)

- Designate a member of the administrative team or seek a staff volunteer to coordinate the assembly and special events programme.
- Involve pupils and school groups in planning, presenting, performing and evaluating. Remind pupils about behaviour expected in formal large groups; refer to the code of conduct.
- Select a yearly theme or activities that support the school's wider curriculum or school improvement plan.
- Post events on the weekly announcements and yearly planning calendar.
- Wherever possible, involve the whole pupil body or different year and multi-age groups. Invite guests from the community (for example, a pensioner, a local author or artist, a former pupil, a police officer).
- Use video conferencing to connect pupils with real-time events.
- Monitor carefully entertainment events and school social/cultural activities to ensure that they support a positive school climate and have educational value, and that the risk to the health and safety of the pupils is minimal.

Performances, concerts, dances and special events (evenings and weekends)

1. Adults must supervise all events; a senior member of the school staff should always be present at a special event.

   (a) Evening events such as dances, competitions, fashion shows, quiz nights, and so on may require additional security support. Follow your local authority's procedures and make sure you have the necessary licences issued by the local authority.
   (b) Review school expectations with the local authority and local community, and deal with any concerns about the safety of pupils at the event.
   (c) Expectations and standards for supervision, health and safety, and behaviour at a dance or social event that takes place at an off-site location are identical to those for an in-school event. Different or extra management provision will have to be made, however, as the event is not on 'home territory' and there may be unforeseen eventualities that are more difficult to manage.

2. Establish a dress code and ensure pupil understanding of the code of conduct.

   (a) For dances and other school events, use of alcohol and tobacco will need deciding and articulating, and drugs must be prohibited. Follow local authority policies and procedures and the code of conduct. Have a plan for how you will respond to misconduct.
   (b) When a pupil or a guest violates the code of conduct, call parents/guardians and arrange for the pupil to return home. Consider the safety and liability of all concerned when making these arrangements.

3. Establish appropriate procedures for admission to such events to ensure proper supervision and safety.
4. If food is served at the event, recognize that some participants may have food allergies and observe the rules for food safety.

Field trips and off-site activities

Preparation

Administrative essentials

- Follow all local authority policies and procedures. If you do not find the elements listed below in your local authority's procedures, consider them when preparing for field trips.

- There are risks for the health and safety of pupils on all field trips. Some trips, such as a visit to a local museum, may be considered low risk; others, such as downhill skiing or foreign travel, are considered high-risk events. If you are uncertain about the risks involved, consult the management of the site of the proposed field trip, your local authority off-site education adviser, and another headteacher whose school has participated in the activity under consideration.
- If an accident occurs on a field trip, follow your local authority's reporting procedures.
- Review the nature of the trip and any issues related to training, transportation, health, safety, special pupil needs, costs and fund-raising.
- Visit the site for a reconnaissance beforehand. Teachers or the headteacher should visit the site (when practical) before the trip to determine learning activities, safety hazards and special requirements.
- Review in advance the list of participating pupils with the staff who are going on a trip.
- Ensure that pupils with special needs are accommodated. On occasion, it may be appropriate to exclude a pupil or pupils. Determine the procedure and criteria for exclusion and publish them well in advance to all participants and parents. They should be the same criteria as used for excluding a pupil from an on-site educational activity. Be aware that any exclusion may be challenged and be ready to give clearly articulated reasons for the decision.
- Provide a list of participating pupils and information about the date and time of the trip in advance to all staff to facilitate their planning.
- Establish a process for cancellation or postponement, in case of inclement weather or unexpected events.
- Write thank you notes to staff, persons who assisted with the visit at the site, financial sponsors, bus drivers, and so on.

Academic essentials

- Educational outcomes for school activities and field trips must clearly state and support school goals and curriculum implementation. These educational outcomes need to be discussed with the pupils.
- A representative from the field trip site may visit the school to meet the pupils, assist with pre-trip learning activities and identify health and safety hazards.
- Pre-trip and post-trip assignments should be part of the field trip plan.
- The teacher in charge should help pupils develop a set of field trip behaviour standards based on the school's code of conduct.
- Evaluate the trip and share results with pupils, staff, volunteers, the host at the field trip site and the governing body.

> **TIP** Consider attending one or more field trips each year yourself.

Authorization

Check local authority policy to determine the role of the local authority in the authorization process for field trips, school teams and athletic events. Consider the following elements when authorizing field trips:

- Written consent from parents or guardians, or the pupil if he or she is 18 years of age or older, may be required, depending on local authority policy.
- Ensure that there is sufficient information on the form for parents to give 'informed consent'. Use local authority permission forms.
- Before a major excursion or high-risk trip, a meeting should be held with the parents, pupils, staff, volunteers and school administration to review the itinerary, health and safety protocols, criteria for exclusion, standards for behaviour, procedures for handling inappropriate behaviour, contact information and any other matters pertinent to the event. Parents should also receive this information in writing.
- Ensure that parents understand that if a pupil is sent home for inappropriate behaviour, it will be equivalent to an official 'exclusion'.

Supervision by staff and other adults, for example, volunteers and family members

- All staff must have appropriate qualifications, and the ratio of pupils to staff and adults must be consistent with the local authority policy.
- Information about medical needs of pupils, home and workplace telephone numbers of parents or guardians, and so on, must be retained by the trip leader and also at the school.
- A procedure for dealing with a medical emergency while on the trip must be established, including any insurance aspects.
- An attendance count should be taken at all points of departure.
- At least one adult from the school and on-site staff should hold current first aid certificates.
- For overnight trips involving male and female pupils, the school staff and adults should be adults of both sexes. Also, staff should be sensitive to

issues that may arise for pupils regarding sexual orientation, disability, cultural or religious observances, and so on.

- Staff/adults should have mobile phones, walkie-talkies, first aid kits and name tags.
- Staff/adults should always designate a location to which pupils must return if they become separated from the group.

Costs

- Field trips and off-site activities' costs should be reasonable and planned for in advance. If the eventual combination of delegated funds and voluntary donations does not cover the full cost of the trip, the trip will have to be cancelled.
- Funds collected for a field trip or an excursion must be deposited in the school account and accounted for at the end of the event.
- Money should never be left anywhere other than the school safe or the bank.
- If the trip does not take place, any voluntary contributions must be repaid.
- Leisure and recreational activities, that are not part of the taught curriculum and educational provision, must be fully funded by the participants and must not be subsidized by the delegated budget.

Transportation

- Prepare copies of a sheet listing the pupils, volunteers and staff riding in each vehicle. One copy is to accompany the staff of each vehicle and one is to be left at the school before departure.
- Use only local authority-approved or reputable transport providers.
- Volunteers, staff and pupils should be discouraged from transporting pupils in their own vehicles. Check your local authority policy. If own cars are used, check insurance, road worthiness and booster seats/seat belts. Also check that the driver has a good driving record.

PART 5

Looking After Yourself

29 Professional Learning and Personal Well-being

An overview: professional learning

Be sure to continue with your professional development activities now that you are a headteacher. Although you are very busy, you still need to make time for your professional learning. It is good for your personal well-being, and it is important to model lifelong learning for pupils and staff.

Remember, you cannot be an expert in everything all at once. Set a focus for yourself and establish your priorities over a three- to five-year cycle.

Make sure that your professional learning needs are recognized by the governing body.

School leadership team

Build a positive working relationship with your deputy and assistant head-teacher(s). Meet regularly to discuss day-to-day operations. Be sure to build in time for mutual professional growth; discuss research trends, teaching/learning strategies or leadership literature. Learn from each other's strengths; share constructive feedback. The deputy headteacher is the only individual in the school with whom you can share certain information and discuss particular situations. Building a supportive professional relationship will reduce the isolation and provide an ongoing opportunity for meaningful professional growth.

> Those who do not reflect lose sight of the fact that their everyday reality is only one of many possible alternatives. They tend to forget the purposes and ends toward which they are working.
>
> (adapted from Grant and Zeichner, 1984)

Professional portfolios

Although the role of headteacher is demanding and offers a considerable number of varied learning opportunities, it is still important to keep a focused perspective on personal professional growth. One of the best ways of achieving this perspective is to maintain a professional portfolio.

There are essentially three major types of professional portfolios, each of which, although different in structure, intent and audience, offers important opportunities for self-reflection and the determination of future personal professional development activities. In preparing these portfolios the headteacher takes the time to reflect upon accomplishments, growth, competencies and needs, and puts current and future actions into a clearer perspective.

Personal growth portfolios

These are the most loosely structured and comprehensive of the three types. They are designed to suit the needs of the individual, to provide opportunities for self-reflection and personal planning, to outline statements of philosophy, to record experiences, to demonstrate competencies and accomplishments, and to set future goals and courses of action.

Personal growth portfolios are intended for use by the author who also may choose to share them with trusted colleagues or coaches.

Evaluation portfolios

These are kept to identify statements of philosophy and goals, and to document those events, experiences and competencies that are stressed by the employer or course provider in order to demonstrate progress and proficiency in the position. Evaluation portfolios are structured to reflect the guidelines or expectations articulated by the employer or course provider and are used during periods of assessment to demonstrate competence and excellence.

They are principally intended for use by an evaluator.

Promotion portfolios

These are developed to demonstrate relevant personal philosophies, proficiency and preparedness for a specific desired position, and are semi-structured in that they are organized to reflect the values and requisite competencies of the organization and the position desired; yet there is some personal latitude in the way in which they are designed.

They are intended for use by a prospective employer.

✅ As varied as these types of portfolios may be, there is much content that is common to all. Portfolios usually contain the following common components in one form or another:

- a table of contents
- a statement of philosophy and goals
- a current résumé
- artefacts (materials produced during normal completion of the job)
- productions (materials produced for the purpose of the portfolio)
- narratives (explanations of significance for each artefact and production)
- attestations and accolades
- professional development records
- community involvement records.

The maintenance of a professional portfolio is an individual, fluid activity involving many personal choices regarding structure, format and content. This activity provides very important opportunities for self-reflection, setting goals, recording accomplishments and accolades, outlining a history of growth, demonstrating competencies, outlining future courses of action, and clarifying your purpose, philosophy and practice. A professional portfolio demonstrates where you have been, the current context of your position, and a focus and direction for the future.

Further reading

Brown, G. and Irby, B.J. (2001) *The Principal Portfolio.*

Conferences

Keep up to date on conferences being offered. Don't just assume that you cannot go due to funding or time constraints. If you find a conference that meets your needs and fits in with your professional goals, think creatively about how you might be able to arrange attendance.

Workshops and training sessions

Take part in professional development and other practical training opportunities offered by your local authority or professional association for new school headteachers.

Mentors

Identify an experienced headteacher in the local authority who is willing to act as your mentor. This may be an individual mentor, or it may be a cohort mentor who is working with a small group of new headteachers. If the local authority has a formal mentoring programme, take part in it.

Discuss with your mentor mutual goals for the mentoring relationship, a meeting schedule, strategies for communication between meetings, your particular issues of concern (for example, budget), records to be kept (for example, a professional journal), and other questions. Build in a review process.

Networking

Attend regional and local meetings for headteachers and deputy headteachers, local workshops and training sessions, and local professional meetings.

Form a support group that includes new and experienced colleagues, or form a support group composed solely of new headteachers; these are sometimes referred to as co-mentoring groups. Have breakfast or lunch with colleagues. Informal networking is invaluable; don't skip it. Form electronic networking groups.

Create work groups to complete tasks collaboratively, especially for those jobs that all headteachers share. These are sometimes referred to as round table sessions, where common assignments can be completed with colleagues and an expert local coach, combining professional development and task completion.

At the very least, develop a personal roster of local experts to call, prior to finalizing important decisions, especially if you are working in isolation.

Personal code of conduct

Develop your own personal code of conduct. Review and revise it from time to time.

- Maintain absolute integrity in all things at all times.
- Praise in public; criticize in private.
- Treat your word as bond; keep your promises.
- Always be on time.
- Accept responsibility for your actions.

Source: adapted from Crittendon, 2002, p. 16.

📖 Professional reading

Look for professional articles and books that give practical advice to new school leaders. Set priorities; you cannot do everything all at once. Give yourself credit for the aspects of your work that you already have under control. The list below gives titles of some recommended works and outlines their contents.

Getting Through Year One by Joan Daly-Lewis

1. The staff:

   If it works, don't fix it.
   Fight the jump reflex.
   Let go; delegate.

2. The work:

   Get to know the culture of your school and local authority. View the year in terms of functional seasons.
   Leave footprints.

3. Personal survival:

    Seek a mentor, confidant, and adviser.
    Identify and consult with the team leaders.
    Don't take yourself or others too seriously.

**'A letter to newly appointed headteachers: ten tips for
making the grade' by Kevin Skelly**

1. Understand the power of the position.
2. Have a mentor.
3. Listen.
4. Be humble.
5. Do something safe, dramatic and visible early.
6. Find out as much as possible about your predecessors and where the
    land mines are.
7. Ask people for advice on how to make decisions, and move slowly to
    change existing policies.
8. Be an educational leader.
9. Be positive.
10. Keep things in perspective.

**'Starting on the right foot: a blueprint for incoming principals' by Lawrence
Roder and David Pearlman**

1. Designing an entry plan.
2. Finding out what matters: get to know the school and community.
3. The job versus the job description.

Ten Principles for New Principals: A Guide to Positive Action by Mark Joel

1. Change is constant.
2. A headship is a power position.
3. First impressions are lasting impressions.
4. All things are not created equal.
5. Allow other lights to shine.
6. People share their interpretation of your message.
7. The buck stops here.
8. Together is better.
9. Accountability counts.
10. Work smarter.

The 7 Habits of Highly Effective People by Stephen Covey

1. Be proactive.
2. Begin with the end in mind.
3. Put first things first.
4. Think win-win.
5. Seek first to understand, then to be understood.
6. Synergize.
7. Sharpen the saw.

'What makes a leader?' by Daniel Goleman
The five components of emotional intelligence at work:

1. Self-awareness.
2. Self-regulation.
3. Motivation.
4. Empathy.
5. Social skill.

Personal well-being

 Stress management: a questionnaire

You have a very demanding job. Be sure to monitor your workload and behaviour and the impact they are having on your body. Start by answering the following questions:

- Do you get a knot in your stomach, headaches, or other physiological sensations at work or while thinking about work?
- Does your heart race on Sunday night thinking about work and what you have to do tomorrow?
- Are you missing out on social, family or personal occasions because of work?
- Do you put off medical and dental appointments because you are too busy?
- Does time off, such as vacations, cause more stress than working?
- When you are off, do you have difficulty leaving the work behind?
- Do you feel like a martyr as you tell others how much overtime you have put in?
- Does being at work make you feel better than being anywhere else?
- Do you feel pressure from colleagues or superiors to work longer and later because they do?

- Do you have the expectation that others should keep the pace and hours you choose to keep?

Source: adapted from Beresford, 2002, pp. 30–3.

Depending on your responses to these questions, you may want to take a closer look at your priorities. Perhaps you would benefit from trying to put some balance back into your life or from practising some stress management techniques as described below.

Ten suggestions for reducing stress

1. Allow time for relaxation, hobbies, sports, television, vacations.
2. Rest is essential. Have a nap; go to bed early.
3. Regular meals are essential as well. Don't skip breakfast or lunch.
4. Start to work out; you will decrease stress.
5. Humour does wonders. Lighten up at home and at school.
6. What you model sets a tone that can contribute to the guilt that other staff members may feel. Do not reward overwork.
7. Keep your hours at school, and at home, reasonable.
8. Do not feel guilty when you leave work early (which for most people is really on time) to attend meaningful events in your personal life.
9. Don't allow your work alone to define you.
10. Define yourself by your ability to balance work-related stress.

Source: Beresford, 2002, pp. 30–3.

Note: No amount of reading will, by itself, reduce your stress or add balance to your life. Picking just one item from the above list, and changing your behaviour in that one area, will make a difference.

Personal resilience is a key to a successful career as a school leader

'Headteachers need to accept that change is ongoing, that they alone are responsible for their attitudes, that they have control of their lives, that their ongoing learning is important to working smarter, and that they need to take time to reflect on their successes.'

(Joel, 2002, p. 63)

Know where to get help

If you are dealing with excessive stress, know where to get assistance:

- your professional association for professional advice and assistance
- the local authority's employee assistance programme
- your family doctor.

LOOK AFTER YOURSELF
Maintaining balance between your personal and professional life is essential. Not only is it healthy for you as an individual, but it also sends a positive message to your staff. Be fit. Begin a physical fitness programme and eat properly. Take time for yourself to relax and re-energize.

30 Support for School Leaders

At a glance

- What to do when you need help
- When to call your professional association for assistance

What to do when you need help

When you are dealing with a difficult situation or a crisis, it is essential to consult others. Discuss the matter with the following people:

1. deputy headteacher
2. chair of governors
3. professional association
4. mentor
5. colleagues
6. other experts in your local area
7. other professionals, as appropriate.

When you are dealing with a particularly difficult situation, call your professional association for advice, assistance and support.

When to call your professional association for assistance

Be sure to call your professional association and ask to speak with the appropriate officer when:

- you have a management issue, in general, which the association may be able to advise you on

- your own position as headteacher is under scrutiny or threat as a result of personnel procedures against you or grievances/complaints against you
- you are served with legal papers related to your role as a headteacher
- you are dealing with particularly challenging parents
- you are called as a witness
- you are contemplating staff discipline
- there are complaints or accusations against you from union members
- you are having difficulty with your local authority or deputy headteacher or governors
- you are facing investigation by your local authority
- questions arise about long-term disability, pension, retirement, leave of absence, redundancy, salary and conditions of service.

> When there has been a serious accident, or you are dealing with a school crisis, or there is significant media involvement, take all the appropriate first steps according to local authority procedures.
>
> Your local authority should have a disaster planning team and a press/public relations section.

CALL ON COLLEAGUES; BUILD A NETWORK

Asking someone's advice is a sincere form of flattery.

Build a support network.

Attend any professional association workshops that you can; they provide valuable and useful information on how to do the job.

31 Words of Wisdom

At a glance

- Advice from new headteachers
- Activities and checklists

  Regular monthly activities for headteachers
  Getting the school year started: checklists for July, August and September

Advice from new headteachers

These words of advice come from first and second year primary and secondary headteachers. Their advice has been clustered into 12 categories, which are presented in random order below. Here is what new headteachers said in their own words. Consider how this advice can help you.

1. You're not in this by yourself

- It's wise to ask for advice.
- There are people who would love to have you ask their opinions; for example, more experienced colleagues in your local authority.
- Network with your colleagues regularly.
- Find a confidant, a mentor. You can't talk to the staff and community about everything. Find someone you can share your doubts with; find a colleague you can talk to in order to make sure you're on track.
- Identify resource people you can rely on at the local authority and elsewhere.
- Work closely with your school business manager or bursar or secretary who probably has a wealth of information about the school and the community. Seek their advice; value their expertise; meet with them regularly. Delegate tasks as appropriate.

- Train your secretary to organize you so that you retain a strategic focus and do not get overly involved in day-to-day minutiae.

2.   You don't have to make decisions this minute

- You need to know when to tell people you'll get back to them after you get further information.
- Things are not always as they appear.
- Make sure you have all the facts.
- In a few words … 'trust but verify!'

3.   Don't try to change everything all at once

- Respect the history and culture of the school.
- Know your community.
- Find a couple of key staff members to run ideas by before putting a new model out for general comment from the entire staff.
- Do thermometer checks with the staff. Seek feedback. Use focus groups.

4.   Don't expect to know all the answers, because you won't

- Nor should you, colleagues are being paid to know many of the answers, your job is more about asking the right questions.
- Every day brings new experiences.
- Constantly re-evaluate your daily priorities.

5.   Have a positive attitude

- Be enthusiastic. Your mood impacts on the staff.
- If there is a situation to be complained about, make sure you focus on the possible solutions and options that there will always be, to resolve the situation.

6.   Keep your focus during negative situations

- Learn to trust your inner voice and what it tells you about what's right, what's wrong, and what's worth fighting for. Pick your fights carefully.

- Look further forward to what will be the likely knock-on effect if either you win or lose the 'fight'.
- Know your values. Make decisions with the students in mind and then you'll be able to live with your decisions.
- Depersonalize staff reactions to your decisions. Don't let staff issues keep you awake at night. Don't spend ages wondering why people act as they do.
- Unless it's absolutely critical, don't agonize; most of your worries will never come to fruition.
- Deal with human resources issues in a timely manner; don't put them off, or small problems will become big ones. People need active management and leadership.

7. Remember, it's a team effort

- Promote teamwork and shared decision-making.
- Don't ask for input if you are not going to listen.
- Don't forget what it was like to be a teacher ... headteachers may not be the best teachers but as the lead professional they should be at least seen as very capable.
- Recruit people with information and communication technology skills.
- Acknowledge the good things people do.
- Write thank you notes.
- Organize and support staff social functions; work together to help a good cause.
- Delegate appropriate tasks, even if you do not have an administration team or deputy. Match the task with the individual. Delegate the authority as well as the responsibility.
- Share leadership opportunities.
- Enjoy your job and pass that enjoyment along. Cultivate future leaders.

8. Be visible

- Try to keep in touch with initiatives in the classrooms, but remember you can't know everything.
- Tell staff you want to see students and their work. Welcome students to your office.
- You are assuming the office previously held by another person. Does the office reflect you? Do you meet people across a desk, at a round table, in large chairs? Your office sends a message. Is your office filled with out-of-date clutter, or is it focused on current issues and children's work?

9. Don't be afraid to leave your school

- Graveyards are full of people who thought they could not be replaced.
- Let staff know that generally you will be available either before school or after school, but don't extend both ends of your working day.
- Give yourself psychological permission to leave the school when it's appropriate; set a stop time.

10. Take time for your own professional development

- Take advantage of professional development activities, especially practical ones specifically related to your new job.

11. Get ready for the number of hours the job will take

- You think you know what it will be like to be a headteacher, but you don't.
- It's a job that's never done. Do what's urgent. Prioritize tasks. Have a life.
- You can't do it all; you can't get all your work done every day.
- No matter what kind of day you have had, when you get home remember that your family and friends are the most important people.
- Try to avoid being preoccupied at home when those around you need you, and you need them.

12. You need to be aware of the perceptions that others have of 'the headteacher'

- You may not feel any different, but others' reactions to you will be very different.
- You have a public image; you are always on the job.
- Remember that you work for the local authority and you represent the local authority. Even in foundation, voluntary aided and similar schools you represent the local education service.
- Accept the fact that sometimes you'll feel lonely in your leadership role.
- Know your strengths and your weaknesses, and know where you need help. You're not perfect; don't hide your weaknesses.
- Be real. If your word is good, staff will forgive you an error you've made. If you really care about the kids, parents will support you.
- Live what you believe.
- Believe that you are actually the best ... unless you believe it, no one else will!

Termly tasks	Led by whom	Reporting to/ sharing with
1 • Review termly checklist.	HT	SLT
• Know the significant faith dates on the calendar.		TLRs
		Governors
• Plan time for SLT evaluation, review, 'thought showering' and future planning.		Religious Education
• Identify goals and set priorities for the term.		Subject leader
2 • Review budget accounts.	Bursar	HT
• Compile and submit termly reports (e.g., attendance, exclusions).		SLT
		Clerical
• Ensure electronic records and files are backed up.	CA	Assistant
3 • Conduct fire or other emergency drills.	Deputy HT	HT
• Meet with Site Manager; conduct weekly walk-through of accommodation.	Site Manager	
4 • Review progress toward school improvement plan objectives.	HT	SLT
		TLRs
		Whole staff team
5 • Review and follow up regarding pupil behaviour and discipline trends.	Assistant HT	HT
		CA
• Review and follow up regarding pupil achievement statistics.	Deputy HT	TLRs
		Whole staff
	team	
6 • Conduct classroom visits and staff feedback	HT	SLT
• Conduct mentoring sessions and induction meetings with NQTs and new teachers.	Nominated mentors	HT
7 • Prepare weekly bulletins or updates for staff.	HT/SLT	Whole staff
• Draft staff memos.		team
• Write thank you notes.		

Activities		
• Distribute regular termly newsletter and calendar.	*PA*	*Whole school community Pupils*
• Prepare next month's newsletter and calendar.		
• Review pupil newspaper and classroom newsletters.	*Pupil council*	
8 • Review school web page. • Update staffroom notice boards. • Post upcoming events on outdoor display board.	*ICT technician TA team leader*	*HT Bursar/CA Staff Families Pupils*
9 • Conduct staff meeting. • Attend team, department and school committee meetings.	*HT, SLT or TLRS*	*Staff Governors*
10 • Meet with Chair of Governors. • Attend Governors' meeting.	*HT*	*Teacher and staff representatives*
11 • Attend pupil assemblies and special presentations.	*HT*	*SLT*
• Staff and pupil achievement presentations/ assemblies (e.g., pupil of the month).		*Pupil Council staff leader*
• Attend special events: team sports, concerts, etc.		
• Observe Pupil Council meeting.		
12 • Attend Headteacher meetings.	*HT*	*SLT*
• Attend local professional association meeting. Additional termly activities (add your own items here)		
• — • — • —		

✔ Activities and checklists

Regular monthly activities for headteachers

Check your local authority's monthly calendar for school leaders. Also, see Chapter 4, 'Management Skills', for more time management techniques and tips.

Your regular monthly activities may include the items below. Add to this list as the year goes by:

 Getting the school year started: checklists for July, August and September

The following checklists reflect a headteacher's general schedule. Actual monthly calendars will vary from school to school and from local authority to local authority.

As a new headteacher, it is unlikely that you will be in post at this time, although this checklist is useful for acting headteachers and new headteachers in checking that school is ready for the start of the new year in September.

Term 4

March is the time to scan the environment and tactically plan for a smooth start of the new academic year.

1. *Complete hiring and staffing*

    - Know which staff are looking for promotion or resigning or moving to a new post in September.
    - Consult the SDP and the budget about what the school needs to move forward into its next phase of development in order to decide what staffing will aid this – this may look like the current staffing situation or may include alternative forms of provision.
    - Consider your numbers on roll and the class situation for the next year. Think about your school's results and what the outcomes are looking like.
    - Write and place advertisements with deadlines for the return of the application and interview dates included.
    - Prepare job and person specifications as well as information about the school to send to prospective candidates.
    - Consult with the SLT and governors about the style of the advertisement; whether it is going national or local and about who is on the interview panel for shortlisting and interviewing.
    - Complete as much of the recruitment as possible in order to know the structure for September.
    - Prepare information packages for new staff.

Term 5

2. *Induction of new pupils*

    - Devise the induction programme and send letters to incoming Foundation Stage, Year 3 or Year 7 pupils.

3. *Budget*

    - Ensure the governors have authorised the new budget and that it has been submitted to your LA finance officer.
    - Know the development points within your budget so that any additional staffing planned for September has been advertised and timetabled (using the same structure as before) to be in place by the close of the summer term.

Term 6

4. *Review*

    - Consider a whole-school review of the vision/mission statement.
    - Class structures and lists.
    - Allocation of staff to teaching groups.
    - Curriculum and course outlines prepared by staff.
    - School plans (for example, building works scheduled during the summer holidays, in-service training days planned and consultants recruited).
    - School prospectus and staff and pupil handbooks.
    - Complete the leadership and management section of your School Self-Evaluation.
    - Ensure school supplies have been ordered.

5. *Meetings*

    - Ensure you bring everyone in your SLT on board with you.
    - Deputy headteacher, assistant headteacher and middle leaders.
    - Review and revise administrative responsibilities with the finance officer.
    - Review office routines and responsibilities with clerical assistants.
    - Meet the site manager/s to ensure they are supportive of the building goals for the coming year.

- Check all issues to do with health and safety – are risk assessments in place for summer holiday work? Have security arrangements been reviewed?
- This may include meeting local police and fire departments; arrange for school walk-through, if appropriate.
- Complete the performance management cycle in order to inform the targets for next year.

6. *Planning*

- Teacher feedback from exit interviews, staff questionnaires.
- Gather in-house school statistics, including standardized testing results in preparation for planning to raise standards and awareness of the Autumn package including PANDA/RAISE and Fischer Family Trust.
- Consult and devise the school calendar for the coming year including key school events as well as fund-raising and social events.
- Include fire drill schedule in your own personal diary.
- Establish various school committee meeting dates.
- Check DfES website for dates regarding testing and release of results.
- Check your multicultural calendar for significant dates.
- Review schedule of social activities for pupils for the year.
- Enter all pertinent dates on your own calendar.
- Request that the educational visits coordinator uses the curriculum plan to schedule and plan educational visits for all year groups within the coming year.
- Plan fund-raising activities provided by any parent support groups.
- Plan dates for any community group forums and parents' consultation meetings.
- Hold induction meetings with new parents.
- Meet new pupils.
- Ensure hiring and staffing is complete.
- Review staff teaching and learning responsibilities and, where appropriate, review their job descriptions to include precise expectations for the coming year.
- Review the school's transport plan (where necessary).
- Publish information regarding bus schedules.
- Review information regarding bus routes, drivers, and companies and their contact information, addresses, busing issues and concerns.
- Ensure someone has driven the bus routes.
- Review attendance procedures and know the areas that the pupils come from.

- Review the behaviour policies and procedures and ensure everyone has a revised copy.
- Learn how to operate and override fire alarm and security systems.
- Become aware of operations for the heating system, electrical panels, water shutoff, emergency lighting.

7. *School improvement planning*

- Establish goals and projects for the new year.
- Using all the information from the reviews you have gathered prepare the School Improvement Plan annual priorities for the coming year and share this with all staff and governors.
- Include in your planning:
  - special education needs
  - information and communication technology
  - school emergency/crisis response plan
  - effective communication
  - budget allocations
  - continuing professional development of all staff.

8. *Preparing for the first week back – whole staff*

- Review and update individual staff and pupil timetables.
- Ensure preparation time is adequate; check all relevant clauses in the collective agreements for all unions.
- Ensure lockers are appropriately assigned.
- Distribute up to date class lists to teachers.
- Ensure school supplies have arrived.
- Complete timetables for social times such as playtimes, lunchtimes and detentions.
- Review procedures for administration of medication to pupils, knowing who is new to the school and needing medical support.
- Ensure identification badges are ready for new staff.
- Arrange for revised staff handbook to be copied for distribution before the end of the term.
- Ensure all staff (including those new to school) know the school opening times during the holiday period.

9. *Before pupils come into school in the new term*

- Conduct a walk-through with the site manager to check any maintenance works, school cleanliness and learning environments are ready.
- Locate health and safety documentation.

- Practise using all aspects of public address (PA) system.
- Review school hours and bell times.
- Check and test bell signal system.
- Conduct final check of buildings and grounds.

September

'The great thing about each school year is that it gives everyone a chance to renew and to start over with a clean slate. Expectations from parents, pupils, and staff are high. It is the principal's job to ensure that everyone enters this phase of the year optimistically; just as taking off is the most significant and potentially most dangerous part of an airplane's flight, so is September in the school year's progress. Great caution and care must be taken during September to ensure and maintain a great start.'

(Joel, 2002 p. 20)

1. *Welcome returning staff and pupils*

   (a) Welcome individual staff members as they return to school.
   (b) Welcome new pupils and parents as they register.
   (c) Be highly visible.

2. *Schedule first staff meeting within the school's agreement for directed time*

   (a) Prepare welcome and agenda for first staff meeting.
   (b) Prepare September update memo to staff.

3. *Prepare back-to-school communications for pupils, staff, and parents*

   (a) Welcome back letter for staff.
   (b) Newsletter and calendar for distribution to pupils during the first week of school.

4. *Pupil safety*

   (a) Collect pupil medical information and share with appropriate staff.
   (b) Conduct bus safety training for pupils.
   (c) Ensure placement of safety patrollers and crossing guards.

(d) Arrange three fire drills before end of first term.

(e) Review emergency response plans with staff and pupils.

(f) Ensure that a safe arrival program (infant, first and primary schools) is in place.

(g) Conduct school-wide pediculosis check, if appropriate.

5. *Set up meetings with the following people*

(a) Deputy head and assistant head teachers.

(b) Office administrator, secretary or administrative assistant.

(c) TLR leaders of projects, year groups, departments or teams.

(d) Workplace health and safety representative.

(e) Pupil Council leader.

(f) Chair of governors.

6. *Set up a monitoring and evaluation programme for the year in consultation with SLT and the school self-evaluation process*

(a) Check new staff induction sessions have taken place.

(b) Plan new teacher mentoring programme.

(c) Plan coaching programme for improving staff performance.

(d) Prepare guidance for supply teachers.

7. *Confirm your membership in educational organizations and professional associations*

- Catch up on your professional reading.
- Subscribe to and read professional newspapers.

8. *Attendance*

(a) Report daily attendance and enrollment updates to the SLT team.

(b) Conduct ongoing checks for pupils who were not present at start of the school year.

(c) Complete any month-end reports required by the LA.

9. *Timetables*

(a) Reorganize if necessary; make staffing, timetables and class adjustments as required.

(b) Keep staff and parents informed about any organizational changes.

(c) Ensure that teachers submit final class timetables and copies of curriculum changes.

(d) Ensure everyone is aware of the school's reporting, recording and assessment arrangements.

10. *Staff meetings*

(a) Hold initial staff meeting/regular September staff meeting as per collective agreement.
(b) Schedule staff meetings and department and team meetings.

11. *Governors*

(a) Meet with chair of governors.
(b) Hold first governors' meeting and re-elect officers.
(c) Set dates for year's governors' meetings.

12. *Special education*

(a) Review special education provision and the use of special programmes.
(b) Schedule referral meetings for pupils on School Action and School Action Plus as well as newly registered pupils.
(c) Ensure that IEPs are planned for and reviewed within the month.

13. *School plans*

(a) Update school improvement plan.
(b) Update school calendar and pupil activity calendar.
(c) Reconfirm all dates for scheduled standardized testing and release of results.

14. *Community connection*

(a) Review system of newsletters.
(b) Distribute September newsletter and parent handbook.
(c) Recruit parent volunteers.

15. *Pupil direction*

(a) Distribute pupil handbook.
(b) Establish assembly timetables.
(c) Establish induction programme for new pupils.
(d) Hold pupil assemblies regarding code of conduct and other expectations.

16. *School and home*

   (a) Plan for and hold first Open House Evening (Meet the Teacher Night).
   (b) Confirm schedule for school photos.

17. *Professional development*

   (a) Update staff development plan.
   (b) Plan professional development activities for regular staff meetings (within the school's agreement.)
   (c) Plan for the in-school professional development day.
   (d) Continue new teacher induction program.
   (e) Conduct class visits daily.
   (f) Set up formal classroom visits schedule (within the school's monitoring and evaluating policy).
   (g) Schedule the headteacher performance management meeting with governors.
   (h) Schedule the teacher performance management meetings.
   (i) Re-establish business–education partnerships.

'When you become a principal for the first time, you will face certain issues. One of these is that people will look at you differently, expect different things from you, and hold you accountable in ways that will be markedly different from what they did in the past. Simply stated, you are now "the boss" and this designation carries certain challenges and demands'.

(Daresh, 2001, p. 107)

Resources

The books and websites listed below are presented as a starting point for further reading. Many quality references are available to school leaders, but only a few can be noted here.

 Books

Atkinson, T. and Glaxton, G. (2000) *The Intuitive Practitioner*. Open University Press.

Collins, J. (2001) *From Good to Great*. Random House.

Covey, S. (1992) *The 7 Habits of Highly Effective People*. Simon & Schuster.

Covey, S. (2004) *The 8th Habit*. Simon & Schuster.

Davies, B. (2005) *The Essentials of School Leadership*. Paul Chapman Publishing.

Davis, B. and Ellison, L. (1997) *School Leadership for the 21st Century*. Routledge.

Day, C., Harris, A., Hadfeld M., Tolley, H. and Beresford, J. (2000) *Leading Schools in Times of Change*. Open University Press.

Fullan, M. (1992) *What's Worth Fighting For in Headship*. Open University Press.

Fullan, M. (2001) *Leading in a Culture of Change*. Jossey-Bass.

Fullan, M. (2005) *Leadership and Sustainability*. Open University Press.

Goleman, D. (1996) *Emotional Intelligence*. Bloomsbury.

Goleman, D., Boyatzis, R.E. and McKee, A. (2002) *The New Leaders*. Little, Brown.

Gronn, P. (1999) *The Making of Educational Leaders*. Cassell.

Harris, A. and Bennett, N. (2001) *School Effectiveness and School Improvement*. Continuum.

Jones, J. (2005) *Management Skills in Schools*. Paul Chapman Publishing.

Joyce, B., Calhoun, E. and Hopkins, D. (1999) *The New Structure of School Improvement*. Open University Press.

McCall, C. and Lawler, H. (2002) *Leading and Managing Effective Learning*. Optimum.

Middlewood, D., Parker, R. and Beere, J. (2005) *Creating a Learning School*. Paul Chapman Publishing.

Novak, J. (2002) *Inviting Educational Leadership*. Pearson.

Sallis, J. (2001) *Heads in Partnership. Working with your governors for a successful school*. Pearson.

Tomlinson, H. (2004) *Educational Leadership*. Paul Chapman Publishing.

Websites

British Educational Communications and Technology Agency (BECTA) – **www.becta.org.uk**
BECTA is a UK agency which supports all four UK education departments in their strategic ICT developments. The site provides practical advice, tools and services for leadership teams, teaching staff, technical staff and support providers in schools.

Chartered Institute of Professional Development – www.cipd.co.uk
Human resources and professional development institute.

Criminals Record Bureau – www.crb.gov.uk
Helps organizations by identifying candidates who may be unsuitable to work with children or other vulnerable members of society.

Department for Education and Skills (DfES) – www.dfes.gov.uk
Official site for the governmental department and links to other official sites such as The Standards Site.

Every Child Matters – www.everychildmatters
Official website covering all areas associated with *Every Child Matters: Change for Children*.

General Teaching Council – www.gtce.org.uk
The General Teaching Council – England is the professional body for teaching, and aims to provide an opportunity for teachers to shape the development of professional practice and policy, and to maintain and set professional standards.

Governet – www.governornet.co.uk
Official government site offering up-to-date information on all aspects of school governance.

Local Government Employers (LGE) – www.lg-employers.gov.uk
The LGE works with local authorities, regional employers and other bodies to lead and create solutions on pay, pensions and the employment contract, to ensure the provision of excellent and affordable local services.

NACRO – www.nacro.org.uk
Nacro is an independent voluntary organization working to find practical solutions to reducing and preventing crime.

National Association of Head Teachers – www.naht.org.uk
The NAHT has provided over a century of dedicated support to its members and speaks with authority and strength on educational issues covering early years, primary, secondary and special sectors.

National College for School Leadership – www.ncsl.org.uk
Provides learning and development opportunities and professional and practical support for school leaders. Core purpose is to develop individuals and teams to lead and manage their own schools and work collaboratively with others.

National Confederation of Parent Teacher Associations (NCPTA) – www.ncpta.org.uk
The NCPTA, a registered charity, is the membership organization for Parent Teacher Associations (PTAs) and other home school partnerships throughout England, Wales and Northern Ireland.

National Governors' Association – www.nga.org.uk
The National Governors' Association is a registered charity, established for general public benefit but in particular to improve the educational welfare of children by promoting high standards in schools, and raising the effectiveness of governing bodies.

Office for Standards in Education (Ofsted) – www.ofsted.gov.uk
Ofsted is the inspectorate for children and learners in England, through a comprehensive system of inspection and regulation covering childcare, schools, colleges, children's services, teacher training and youth work. Ofsted will become the Office for Standards in Education, Children's Services and Skills. It will be headed by Her Majesty's Chief Inspector of Education, Children's Services and Skills, and there will be a cohort of Her Majesty's Inspectors of Education, Children's Services and Skills. The organization will retain the existing name of Ofsted, and the inspectors will retain the title of HMI.

Parent Centre – www.parentscentre.gov.uk
Helping you to help your child
Information and support for parents on how to help with your child's learning, including advice on choosing a school and finding childcare.

Supporting Self-evaluation – www.supportingselfevaluation.org.uk
This DfES site includes an interactive self-evaluation tool designed to help leadership teams to assess the stage of development of the school as a whole in selected focus areas.

Teachernet – www.teachernet.gov.uk
The government website for UK teachers and schools-related professions.

References

Alvy, H.B. and Robbins, P. (1998) *If I Only Knew.* Thousand Oaks, CA: Corwin.

Anderson, A. (ed.) (2001) Healthy schools/healthy kids (special issue), *Orbit*, 31(4).

Avery, J. (2002) Conducting effective workplace inspections: identifying hazards that can lead to injury and illness, *The Safe Angle*, 4(1), 3.

Barnett, H. (2001) *Successful K-12 Technology Planning: Ten Essential Elements* (ERIC Document Reproduction Service No. ED45 7858). Retrieved 11 January 2005, from www.eric.ed.gov.

Beresford, L. (2002) Do you stop to smell the roses? *The Register*, 3(4), 30–3.

Brown, A.E. (1998) *Legal Handbook for Educators.* Toronto: Carswell Thomson.

Brown, G. and Irby, B.J. (2001) *The Principal Portfolio.* London: Paul Chapman Publishing.

Covey, S. (1989) *The 7 Habits of Highly Effective People.* New York: Simon & Schuster.

Covey, S., Merrill A. and Merrill, R. (1999) *First Things First.* New York: Simon & Schuster.

Crittendon, R. (2002) *The New Manager's Starter Kit.* New York: AMACOM.

Daly-Lewis, J. (1987) Getting through year one. *Principal*, 67(1), 36–8.

Daresh, J.C. (2001) *Beginning the Principalship.* Thousand Oaks, CA: Corwin.

DfES RR 637 (2005) Creating and sustaining effective professional learning communities.

Fritz, R. (2001) *Think Like a Manager.* Franklin Lakes, NJ: Career Press.

Fullan, M. (1997) *What's Worth Fighting for in a Headship: Strategies for Taking Charge in a Headship.* Open University Press.

Fullan, M. (2001) *Leading in a Culture of Change.* San Francisco, CA: Jossey-Bass.

Fullan, M. (2005) *Leadership and Sustainability.* Thousand Oaks, CA: Corwin; Toronto: Ontario Principals' Council.

Goleman, D. (1995) *Emotional Intelligence.* New York: Bantam.

Goleman, D. (1998a) *Working with Emotional Intelligence.* New York: Bantam.

Goleman, D. (1998b) What makes a leader? *Harvard Business Review*, 71(6), 93–102.

Goleman, D., Boyatzis, R.E. and McKee, A. (2002) *The New Leaders: Transforming the Art of Leadership into the Science of Results.* New York: Little, Brown.

Grant, C.A. and Zeichner, K.M. (1984) *Preparing for Reflective Teaching.* Boston, MA: Allyn & Bacon.

Greene, L.E. (ed.) (2002) Children's health & safety (special issue), *Principal*, 81(5).

Heifetz, R. (1994) *Leadership Without Early Answers.* Cambridge, MA: Harvard University Press.

Joel, M. (2002) *Ten Principles for New Principals: A Guide to Positive Action.* Chicago, IL: Robin Fogarty & Associates.

Jones, J. (2005) *Management Skills in Schools.* London: Paul Chapman Publishing.

Kuhn, H.W. and Nasar, S. (eds) (2001) *The Essential John Nash.* Princeton, NJ: Princeton University Press.

National Association of Elementary School Principals (2001) *Leading Learning Communities: Standards for What Principals Should Know and Be Able to Do.*

A National Framework for Health Promoting Schools (2000–2003). Sydney: Australian Health Promoting Schools Association. Retrieved 11 January 2005, from http://www.hlth.qut.edu.au/ph/ahpsa.

National College for School Leadership (2004) *Distributed Leadership.* Available on www.nacsl.org.uk.

Nelson, B. and Economy, P. (1996) *Managing for Dummies.* Foster City, CA: DG Books.

Newberry, A.J.H. (1996) *A New Time – A New Schoolhouse Leader.* Vancouver: EduServ.

November, A.C. (2001) Managing the transition from paper to light. Presentation to the OPC Odyssey Conference, November, Toronto.

Peterson, K.D. and Deal, T.E. (1998) How leaders influence the culture of schools, *Educational Leadership,* 56(1), 28–30.

Peterson, K.D. and Deal, T.E. (2002) *The Shaping of School Culture Fieldbook.* San Francisco, CA: Jossey-Bass.

Robins, S.L. (2000) *Protecting our Students: Executive Summary and Recommendations.* Toronto: Government of Ontario.

Roder, L. and Pearlman, D. (1989) Starting on the right foot: a blueprint for incoming principals. *NASSP Bulletin,* 73(519), 69–75.

Roher, E.M. and Wormwell, S.A. (2002) *An Educator's Guide to the Role of the Principal.* Aurora: Aurora Professional Press.

Ross, P.N. (1998) *Arresting Violence: A Resource Guide for Schools and Their Communities.* Toronto: Elementary Teachers' Federation of Ontario.

Saphier, J. and King, M. (1984) Good seeds grow in strong cultures. *Educational Leadership,* 42(6), 67–74.

Skelly, K. (1996) A letter to newly appointed principals: ten tips for making the grade. *NASSP Bulletin,* 80(577), 90–6.

Stein, S. and Book, H. (2000) *The EQ Edge.* Toronto: Stoddart.

Stevens, L.J. (2001) *An Administrative Handbook: A View from the Elementary Principal's Desk.* Lanham, MD: Scarecrow Press.

Straub, J.T. (2000) *The Rookie Manager.* New York: Amacom.

Thompson, S.D. (ed.) (1993) *Principals for our Changing Schools, Knowledge and Skill Base.* Lancaster, PA: Technomic.

West-Burnham, J. (2003) *The Handbook of Educational Leadership and Management.* Pearson Longman.

West-Burnham, J. (2004) *Building Leadership Capacity – helping leaders learn.* National College for School Leadership Thinkpiece.

Index